D1562262

AUGUSTUS CAESAR

AUGUSTUS CAESAR

Nancy Zinsser Walworth

CHELSEA HOUSE PUBLISHERS
NEW YORK
PHILADELPHIA

Chelsea House Publishers
EDITOR-IN-CHIEF: Nancy Toff
EXECUTIVE EDITOR: Remmel T. Nunn
MANAGING EDITOR: Karyn Gullen Browne
COPY CHIEF: Juliann Barbato
PICTURE EDITOR: Adrian G. Allen
ART DIRECTOR: Maria Epes
MANUFACTURING MANAGER: Gerald Levine

World Leaders—Past & Present
SENIOR EDITOR: John W. Selfridge

Staff for AUGUSTUS CAESAR:
ASSISTANT EDITOR: Kathleen McDermott
DEPUTY COPY CHIEF: Ellen Scordato
EDITORIAL ASSISTANT: Heather Lewis
PICTURE RESEARCHER: Elie Porter
ASSISTANT ART DIRECTOR: Laurie Jewell
DESIGNER: Ghila Krajzman
PRODUCTION COORDINATOR: Joseph Romano
COVER ILLUSTRATION: Robin Peterson

Copyright © 1989 Chelsea House Publishers, a division of
Main Line Book Co. All rights reserved. Printed and bound in
the United States of America.

First Printing

1   3   5   7   9   8   6   4   2

Library of Congress Cataloging-in-Publication Data

Walworth, Nancy Zinsser.
Augustus Caesar.

(World leaders past & present)
Bibliography: p.
Includes index.
   Summary: A biography of the first Roman emperor, under whom
Rome achieved great glory.

1. Augustus, Emperor of Rome, 63 B.C.–14 A.D.—Juvenile
literature. 2. Rome—History—Civil War, 43–31 B.C.—
Juvenile literature. 3. Rome—History—Augustus, 30
B.C.–14 A.D.—Juvenile literature. 4. Roman emperors—
Biography—Juvenile literature. [1. Augustus, Emperor of
Rome, 63 B.C.–14 A.D. 2. Kings, queens, rulers, etc.
3. Rome—History—Civil.]   I. Title. II. Series.
DG279.W35   1988   937'.07'0924   [B] [92]   88-1113

ISBN 1-55546-804-7

Contents

John Adams
John Quincy Adams
Konrad Adenauer
Alexander the Great
Salvador Allende
Marc Antony
Corazon Aquino
Yasir Arafat
King Arthur
Hafez al-Assad
Kemal Atatürk
Attila
Clement Attlee
Augustus Caesar
Menachem Begin
David Ben-Gurion
Otto von Bismarck
Léon Blum
Simon Bolívar
Cesare Borgia
Willy Brandt
Leonid Brezhnev
Julius Caesar
John Calvin
Jimmy Carter
Fidel Castro
Catherine the Great
Charlemagne
Chiang Kai-Shek
Winston Churchill
Georges Clemenceau
Cleopatra
Constantine the Great
Hernán Cortés
Oliver Cromwell
Georges-Jacques
    Danton
Jefferson Davis
Moshe Dayan
Charles de Gaulle
Eamon De Valera
Eugene Debs
Deng Xiaoping
Benjamin Disraeli
Alexander Dubček
François & Jean-Claude
    Duvalier
Dwight Eisenhower
Eleanor of Aquitaine
Elizabeth I
Faisal
Ferdinand & Isabella
Francisco Franco
Benjamin Franklin

Frederick the Great
Indira Gandhi
Mohandas Gandhi
Giuseppe Garibaldi
Amin & Bashir Gemayel
Genghis Khan
William Gladstone
Mikhail Gorbachev
Ulysses S. Grant
Ernesto "Che" Guevara
Tenzin Gyatso
Alexander Hamilton
Dag Hammarskjöld
Henry VIII
Henry of Navarre
Paul von Hindenburg
Hirohito
Adolf Hitler
Ho Chi Minh
King Hussein
Ivan the Terrible
Andrew Jackson
James I
Wojciech Jaruzelski
Thomas Jefferson
Joan of Arc
Pope John XXIII
Pope John Paul II
Lyndon Johnson
Benito Juárez
John Kennedy
Robert Kennedy
Jomo Kenyatta
Ayatollah Khomeini
Nikita Khrushchev
Kim Il Sung
Martin Luther King, Jr.
Henry Kissinger
Kublai Khan
Lafayette
Robert E. Lee
Vladimir Lenin
Abraham Lincoln
David Lloyd George
Louis XIV
Martin Luther
Judas Maccabeus
James Madison
Nelson & Winnie
    Mandela
Mao Zedong
Ferdinand Marcos
George Marshall

Mary, Queen of Scots
Tomáś Masaryk
Golda Meir
Klemens von Metternich
James Monroe
Hosni Mubarak
Robert Mugabe
Benito Mussolini
Napoléon Bonaparte
Gamal Abdel Nasser
Jawaharlal Nehru
Nero
Nicholas II
Richard Nixon
Kwame Nkrumah
Daniel Ortega
Mohammed Reza Pahlavi
Thomas Paine
Charles Stewart
    Parnell
Pericles
Juan Perón
Peter the Great
Pol Pot
Muammar el-Qaddafi
Ronald Reagan
Cardinal Richelieu
Maximilien Robespierre
Eleanor Roosevelt
Franklin Roosevelt
Theodore Roosevelt
Anwar Sadat
Haile Selassie
Prince Sihanouk
Jan Smuts
Joseph Stalin
Sukarno
Sun Yat-sen
Tamerlane
Mother Teresa
Margaret Thatcher
Josip Broz Tito
Toussaint L'Ouverture
Leon Trotsky
Pierre Trudeau
Harry Truman
Queen Victoria
Lech Walesa
George Washington
Chaim Weizmann
Woodrow Wilson
Xerxes
Emiliano Zapata
Zhou Enlai

CHELSEA HOUSE PUBLISHERS

ON LEADERSHIP

Arthur M. Schlesinger, jr.

LEADERSHIP, it may be said, is really what makes the world go round. Love no doubt smooths the passage; but love is a private transaction between consenting adults. Leadership is a public transaction with history. The idea of leadership affirms the capacity of individuals to move, inspire, and mobilize masses of people so that they act together in pursuit of an end. Sometimes leadership serves good purposes, sometimes bad; but whether the end is benign or evil, great leaders are those men and women who leave their personal stamp on history.

Now, the very concept of leadership implies the proposition that individuals can make a difference. This proposition has never been universally accepted. From classical times to the present day, eminent thinkers have regarded individuals as no more than the agents and pawns of larger forces, whether the gods and goddesses of the ancient world or, in the modern era, race, class, nation, the dialectic, the will of the people, the spirit of the times, history itself. Against such forces, the individual dwindles into insignificance.

So contends the thesis of historical determinism. Tolstoy's great novel *War and Peace* offers a famous statement of the case. Why, Tolstoy asked, did millions of men in the Napoleonic Wars, denying their human feelings and their common sense, move back and forth across Europe slaughtering their fellows? "The war," Tolstoy answered, "was bound to happen simply because it was bound to happen." All prior history predetermined it. As for leaders, they, Tolstoy said, "are but the labels that serve to give a name to an end and, like labels, they have the least possible connection with the event." The greater the leader, "the more conspicuous the inevitability and the predestination of every act he commits." The leader, said Tolstoy, is "the slave of history."

Determinism takes many forms. Marxism is the determinism of class. Nazism the determinism of race. But the idea of men and women as the slaves of history runs athwart the deepest human instincts. Rigid determinism abolishes the idea of human freedom—

the assumption of free choice that underlies every move we make, every word we speak, every thought we think. It abolishes the idea of human responsibility, since it is manifestly unfair to reward or punish people for actions that are by definition beyond their control. No one can live consistently by any deterministic creed. The Marxist states prove this themselves by their extreme susceptibility to the cult of leadership.

More than that, history refutes the idea that individuals make no difference. In December 1931 a British politician crossing Park Avenue in New York City between 76th and 77th Streets around 10:30 P.M. looked in the wrong direction and was knocked down by an automobile—a moment, he later recalled, of a man aghast, a world aglare: "I do not understand why I was not broken like an eggshell or squashed like a gooseberry." Fourteen months later an American politician, sitting in an open car in Miami, Florida, was fired on by an assassin; the man beside him was hit. Those who believe that individuals make no difference to history might well ponder whether the next two decades would have been the same had Mario Constasino's car killed Winston Churchill in 1931 and Giuseppe Zangara's bullet killed Franklin Roosevelt in 1933. Suppose, in addition, that Adolf Hitler had been killed in the street fighting during the Munich *Putsch* of 1923 and that Lenin had died of typhus during World War I. What would the 20th century be like now?

For better or for worse, individuals do make a difference. "The notion that a people can run itself and its affairs anonymously," wrote the philosopher William James, "is now well known to be the silliest of absurdities. Mankind does nothing save through initiatives on the part of inventors, great or small, and imitation by the rest of us—these are the sole factors in human progress. Individuals of genius show the way, and set the patterns, which common people then adopt and follow."

Leadership, James suggests, means leadership in thought as well as in action. In the long run, leaders in thought may well make the greater difference to the world. But, as Woodrow Wilson once said, "Those only are leaders of men, in the general eye, who lead in action. . . . It is at their hands that new thought gets its translation into the crude language of deeds." Leaders in thought often invent in solitude and obscurity, leaving to later generations the tasks of imitation. Leaders in action—the leaders portrayed in this series—have to be effective in their own time.

And they cannot be effective by themselves. They must act in response to the rhythms of their age. Their genius must be adapted, in a phrase of William James's, "to the receptivities of the moment." Leaders are useless without followers. "There goes the mob," said the French politician hearing a clamor in the streets. "I am their leader. I must follow them." Great leaders turn the inchoate emotions of the mob to purposes of their own. They seize on the opportunities of their time, the hopes, fears, frustrations, crises, potentialities. They succeed when events have prepared the way for them, when the community is awaiting to be aroused, when they can provide the clarifying and organizing ideas. Leadership ignites the circuit between the individual and the mass and thereby alters history.

It may alter history for better or for worse. Leaders have been responsible for the most extravagant follies and most monstrous crimes that have beset suffering humanity. They have also been vital in such gains as humanity has made in individual freedom, religious and racial tolerance, social justice, and respect for human rights.

There is no sure way to tell in advance who is going to lead for good and who for evil. But a glance at the gallery of men and women in *World Leaders—Past and Present* suggests some useful tests.

One test is this: Do leaders lead by force or by persuasion? By command or by consent? Through most of history leadership was exercised by the divine right of authority. The duty of followers was to defer and to obey. "Theirs not to reason why / Theirs but to do and die." On occasion, as with the so-called enlightened despots of the 18th century in Europe, absolutist leadership was animated by humane purposes. More often, absolutism nourished the passion for domination, land, gold, and conquest and resulted in tyranny.

The great revolution of modern times has been the revolution of equality. The idea that all people should be equal in their legal condition has undermined the old structure of authority, hierarchy, and deference. The revolution of equality has had two contrary effects on the nature of leadership. For equality, as Alexis de Tocqueville pointed out in his great study *Democracy in America*, might mean equality in servitude as well as equality in freedom.

"I know of only two methods of establishing equality in the political world," Tocqueville wrote. "Rights must be given to every citizen, or none at all to anyone . . . save one, who is the master of all." There was no middle ground "between the sovereignty of all and the absolute power of one man." In his astonishing prediction of 20th-century totalitarian dictatorship, Tocqueville explained how the revolution of equality could lead to the *"Führerprinzip"* and more terrible absolutism than the world had ever known.

But when rights are given to every citizen and the sovereignty of all is established, the problem of leadership takes a new form, becomes more exacting than ever before. It is easy to issue commands and enforce them by the rope and the stake, the concentration camp and the *gulag.* It is much harder to use argument and achievement to overcome opposition and win consent. The Founding Fathers of the United States understood the difficulty. They believed that history had given them the opportunity to decide, as Alexander Hamilton wrote in the first Federalist Paper, whether men are indeed capable of basing government on "reflection and choice, or whether they are forever destined to depend . . . on accident and force."

Government by reflection and choice called for a new style of leadership and a new quality of followership. It required leaders to be responsive to popular concerns, and it required followers to be active and informed participants in the process. Democracy does not eliminate emotion from politics; sometimes it fosters demagoguery; but it is confident that, as the greatest of democratic leaders put it, you cannot fool all of the people all of the time. It measures leadership by results and retires those who overreach or falter or fail.

It is true that in the long run despots are measured by results too. But they can postpone the day of judgment, sometimes indefinitely, and in the meantime they can do infinite harm. It is also true that democracy is no guarantee of virtue and intelligence in government, for the voice of the people is not necessarily the voice of God. But democracy, by assuring the right of opposition, offers built-in resistance to the evils inherent in absolutism. As the theologian Reinhold Niebuhr summed it up, "Man's capacity for justice makes democracy possible, but man's inclination to injustice makes democracy necessary."

A second test for leadership is the end for which power is sought. When leaders have as their goal the supremacy of a master race or the promotion of totalitarian revolution or the acquisition and exploitation of colonies or the protection of greed and privilege or the preservation of personal power, it is likely that their leadership will do little to advance the cause of humanity. When their goal is the abolition of slavery, the liberation of women, the enlargement of opportunity for the poor and powerless, the extension of equal rights to racial minorities, the defense of the freedoms of expression and opposition, it is likely that their leadership will increase the sum of human liberty and welfare.

Leaders have done great harm to the world. They have also conferred great benefits. You will find both sorts in this series. Even "good" leaders must be regarded with a certain wariness. Leaders are not demigods; they put on their trousers one leg after another just like ordinary mortals. No leader is infallible, and every leader needs to be reminded of this at regular intervals. Irreverence irritates leaders but is their salvation. Unquestioning submission corrupts leaders and demeans followers. Making a cult of a leader is always a mistake. Fortunately hero worship generates its own antidote. "Every hero," said Emerson, "becomes a bore at last."

The signal benefit the great leaders confer is to embolden the rest of us to live according to our own best selves, to be active, insistent, and resolute in affirming our own sense of things. For great leaders attest to the reality of human freedom against the supposed inevitabilities of history. And they attest to the wisdom and power that may lie within the most unlikely of us, which is why Abraham Lincoln remains the supreme example of great leadership. A great leader, said Emerson, exhibits new possibilities to all humanity. "We feed on genius. . . . Great men exist that there may be greater men."

Great leaders, in short, justify themselves by emancipating and empowering their followers. So humanity struggles to master its destiny, remembering with Alexis de Tocqueville: "It is true that around every man a fatal circle is traced beyond which he cannot pass; but within the wide verge of that circle he is powerful and free; as it is with man, so with communities."

1

The Soothsayer

The Greek astrologer looked closely at the two young Roman officers who had climbed upstairs to his studio. They were in their late teens and seemed to be close friends, yet they were an odd pair. One was thick-necked and muscular, with rough manners — a farmer's son, perhaps. The other was slim, almost frail, with the smooth manners of the Roman upper class.

The astrologer was used to off-duty Roman soldiers strolling into the town of Apollonia from the huge military base nearby. They were a noisy, restless lot, training in northern Greece that winter of early 44 B.C. while waiting impatiently for their general, Julius Caesar, to leave the city of Rome and lead them against the warlike Parthians in the east.

But these two were different from the usual rowdy soldiers, and the astrologer hoped that the stars might at last reveal something interesting. He asked for the birth date of the larger boy, assuming him

Tales such as these [the astrology story], which so far as history was aware, were not made public until after Octavius attained supreme power, scarcely deserve serious attention; but they are especially interesting in the case of one who . . . firmly believed he was the favourite of Heaven.
—JOHN B. FIRTH
English historian

When politician and general Julius Caesar invaded the Italian peninsula in 44 B.C., he dealt a fatal blow to the 700-year-old Roman republic. He did not live long enough, however, to introduce a new political order. That task was left to his grandnephew Octavian — the future emperor Augustus.

A 2nd-century A.D. Roman historian, Gaius Suetonius Tranquillus wrote biographies of several Roman emperors. Suetonius recorded that a Greek astrologer told Octavian, then a sickly, quiet boy, that he would one day become master of the entire Roman world.

to be the leader of the two. Then he consulted books and charts while making mysterious computations. He looked impressed. Turning to the 19-year-old Marcus Vipsanius Agrippa, the astrologer said that he foresaw a remarkable career for him, so remarkable, in fact, that he found it hard to believe.

Agrippa was pleased. He motioned to his friend, Octavian, saying that it was now his turn.

But Octavian started to leave. He was sure that his future could never compare with that of Agrippa, who was such a good athlete and soldier, so strong and confident, that he was bound to become a great general, senator, or even *consul* — the highest elective office in the Roman state. Octavian, by contrast, was neither athletic nor military-minded; in fact, he detested contact sports, and the thought of physical combat made him ill. Surely, he thought, a Roman with these characteristics would have no future at all. He started down the stairs of the astrologer's studio, but his friend pulled at his cloak and finally persuaded him to take his turn.

Octavian reluctantly gave the astrologer his birth date, September 23, 18 years earlier. The astrologer studied Octavian's face, then turned to his books and charts. His face grew troubled. He went over his calculations again to be sure he had not made a mistake.

Then, to Octavian's astonishment, the astrologer suddenly rose from his seat and threw himself face-down at the boy's feet. Finally, when he was able to speak, he told Octavian that one day he would be master of the Roman world.

This story was told by a Roman historian, Suetonius, who was born a century later but had access to many archives and memoirs, now lost. The ac-

Roman soldiers from the republican period. Although the republic had long been in decline, both the ruling classes and the common people of Rome clung to its ancient political traditions, making it difficult for any ruler to introduce new ideas.

count of the soothsayer may have been embroidered, but his prophecies are historical fact. Agrippa became a famous admiral, general, senator, consul—and right-hand man of the emperor.

And Octavian became the emperor. Later he was renamed Augustus Caesar by a grateful nation after he saved it from anarchy and dissolution. His rule became known as the Augustan Age — one of the great ages in the history of mankind.

Gaius Octavius, known in English as Octavian, was born in 63 B.C. or, according to the Roman calendar of that time, in the 690th year after the founding of the city of Rome. His father, also named Gaius Octavius, was a senator and served in the important

By the 1st century B.C., the Forum was the busy commercial, administrative, and social center of Rome. One of the oldest sections of the city, the Forum had begun as a market and meeting place for the early Romans.

position of *praetor* — state magistrate — in 61 B.C. His mother, Atia, came from a family that had produced several senators.

Rome had come a long way in 700 years, and every Roman in Octavian's day was aware of its glorious history. Starting as a village of Latin warriors on an Italian hilltop, Rome swallowed up the rest of Italy and then swept on to conquer or control all the lands around the edge of the Mediterranean Sea. For the first 250 years of its existence Rome had been ruled by kings. In 509 B.C. the last king, the tyrannical Tarquin the Proud, was driven out by a group of nobles who, using the watchword "liberty!", created the Roman republic.

A *tribune* of the people was one of the most powerful of Rome's elected officials. Originally introduced to protect the interests of the common people, the office of the tribune could not be held by members of the senatorial class.

From then on the word "king" was odious to all the Roman people. Instead, every year they elected two men as *consuls*, or chief executives — each consul able to check the power of the other. The voters also elected senators to write the laws of the land. These officials were expected to have earned their election through years of army and government service. In addition, the people elected their own magistrates, called *tribunes*, who could propose laws to protect civil rights, and, more important, annul any law by crying out *Veto!* — "I forbid!" Many men of exceptional ability were produced under this system.

For more than four centuries the Roman republic was a model of government under the law, a system of checks and balances unique in its day. The famous initials *SPQR* — the Latin acronym for "the Senate and the People of Rome" — were proudly inscribed on buildings and monuments for everyone in the growing republic to see.

By the 1st century B.C. — the century in which Octavian was born — the republic had begun to decline. The powerful upper classes gradually split up in bitter rivalries. Provincial governors and military commanders on the frontiers became increasingly rich, powerful, and all too often, corrupt. Political power became concentrated in the hands of these men, who cared nothing for the real interests of their country. Seeking votes, they bribed the poor of the city with money, food, and extravagant free spectacles such as chariot races, gladiatorial combats, and wild beast shows.

An ominous note sounded in 83 B.C. when an ambitious army commander, Lucius Cornelius Sulla, marched his troops against his fellow citizens and became, for a time, a bloody and cruel dictator. He ordered a "proscription," a method of getting rid of his enemies by proclaiming them outlaws, putting a price upon their heads, and displaying their names on tablets in the public Forum, the political and social center of Rome. Some of these outlaws were merely very wealthy men whose money Sulla needed to pay his soldiers. Sulla resigned his dictatorship after a year, but he had further weakened the republic. His illegal practices and his use of the army as a political weapon set a dangerous precedent. It was now apparent to many people that the old Roman constitution, with its safeguards against unjust seizure of power, had been undermined and might not be able to hold out much longer against the will and ambition of dangerous men.

One such ambitious man was Julius Caesar, a brilliant and subtle aristocrat. Lucky to survive Sulla's wrath, he took up politics in Rome and learned that he could rouse men's minds and manipulate them for his own uses. Teaming up with another

Every Roman battle standard bore the letters SPQR, which stood for *Senatus Populusque Romanus* (the Senate and the people of Rome). The initials, symbolizing shared power under the republic, were engraved upon public buildings, monuments, and official documents.

This Roman relief shows gladiators prepared for battle in an arena. Staging gladiatorial contests was one way that the ruling class kept the favor of the *plebs*, or common people of Rome.

aristocrat, Marcus Licinius Crassus — a man so wealthy that he was said to have put a diamond necklace on an eel in his fish pond — Caesar began in earnest to ascend the political ladder.

In 63 B.C. — the year of Octavian's birth — Caesar was 37 years old and had just secured the prominent office of *Pontifex Maximus*, the chief priest of Rome. A few years later he became governor of a province in Spain. Returning to Rome, he teamed up again with his rich friend Crassus and also with the popular military commander Gnaeus Pompeius, known as Pompey the Great. They formed what came to be called the First Triumvirate (an alliance of three men) — able to pull strings, pay bribes, and influence votes. Through these means Caesar was elected consul in 59 B.C. When his year's term was over, he used his political clout to secure the prestigious governorship of Transalpine Gaul (the

The Roman republic began to decline rapidly toward the end of the 2nd century B.C. when individuals began to use force to secure office. When Gaius Marius (shown here at the destruction of Carthage, Africa) used his troops to secure control of Rome in 107 B.C., he set an ominous precedent for military intervention in the government.

coastal area of southern France). It was here that Caesar, at 41, began his meteoric ascent to glory.

Any other Roman governor might have merely settled down and occupied himself with routine matters in this beautiful and fertile province — but not Caesar. He cast an ambitious eye at the land north of his narrow province and at the turbulent barbarians inhabiting it, who were themselves threatened by the invasions of other barbarians. To Caesar the situation was an open invitation to intervene. For eight years he fought the tribes of Gaul, sweeping from the Atlantic Ocean to the English Channel to the Rhine River, sharing every hardship and taking every risk. He paid his soldiers well and gave them large shares of the rich spoils of war. He also sent huge quantities of booty, slaves, and prisoners back to Rome. Caesar and his conquests became the talk of Rome, and although most people praised him, some began to fear his growing power and popularity.

Octavian was a small, sickly five year old when Caesar first embarked on his conquest of Gaul. The news of Caesar's sensational victories had special meaning for Octavian because he was related to this famous man: His mother, Atia, was Caesar's niece. He must have bragged about the deeds of his granduncle to his playmates and tried to lead them in war games on the playground — although too much activity would send him coughing and wheezing to his bed. In his sickroom he must have daydreamed that one day he would outgrow his spells of ill health and that great Caesar would summon him to his side.

There was something magnetic about Octavian. From his early childhood people were drawn by his intelligence, his calm and mild expression, and his sense of purpose, unusual for his years. In spite of

Julius Caesar (top right) leads his troops in the invasion of Britain in 55 B.C. Caesar was unsuccessful in his attempt to conquer Britain, but his brilliant leadership during the Gallic Wars and consequent subjugation of Gaul (modern France) brought him fame and power in Rome.

Queen Cleopatra of Egypt captivated Julius Caesar when he met her in 48 B.C. Caesar, who was by then virtually the sole ruler of Rome, lived with Cleopatra in the royal palace at Alexandria, Egypt, where she bore him a son, Caesarion.

ill health, he carried himself gracefully and was unusually handsome, with bright eyes, tousled blond hair, and a fine, slightly curved nose. His stepfather, Lucius Marcius Philippus (Octavian's father had died when his son was four years old), was extremely fond of him and brought famous teachers to his country house outside of Rome so that the boy could have the finest classical education. Octavian did particularly well in rhetoric, a subject that taught him to put his thoughts in order, write them down clearly, and speak easily in public. He showed his mastery of the subject at the age of 12, when he gave a funeral oration in honor of his grandmother, Caesar's sister, before a crowd of mourners.

Ambition ran in Octavian's blood. His father, at the time of his death, had been a sure candidate for a consulship. His mother was also ambitious. She knew that Caesar had neither son nor grandson and that his only male descendants were three grandnephews — her son Octavian and the two grandsons of Caesar's older sister. Family ties were especially important to upper-class Romans. Surely Caesar — who traced his blue-blooded lineage back to the founders of Rome — could be expected one day to show interest in his youngest male descendant, Octavian.

A young man receives a white toga — the flowing robe worn by all men of the Roman upper class — in the ceremony that marks his coming of age. After receiving his white toga at the age of 16, Octavian was eager to join his granduncle Julius Caesar on military expeditions.

Caesar returned from Gaul when Octavian was 14. Warned by spies that his former colleague Pompey and others were conspiring against him, he followed the example of the dictator Sulla and marched his armies into the city of Rome. His political enemies fled the country at his swift approach. Caesar soon pursued them — to Greece, to Egypt, to the Black Sea — and returned victorious to Rome two years later.

It was at this time that he had his first good look at his grandnephew Octavian, probably at a gathering of his aristocratic clan, where Atia presented her son to the man who had always been his hero.

Caesar was immediately attracted to Octavian. He had a very discerning eye when it came to recognizing ability. After looking over his two older grandnephews, he decided that they were mediocre, but in Octavian he saw something that others may not have seen—the potential for leadership.

Caesar spent two hectic months in Rome trying to put its inefficient government in order. He did not have much time to spend with Octavian, but he kept an eye on him, liked what he saw, and planned to take him along on his next campaign to give him his first military experience, necessary to every young Roman. When news came that some remaining followers of his old enemy Pompey were fomenting rebellion in the Roman province of Africa, a small strip of coastal land across the sea from Sicily, Caesar planned one of his swift punitive expeditions and invited Octavian along. To Octavian's intense disappointment, Atia put her foot down, saying that he was too young. This was not entirely true, for he was 16 — the age when a young Roman first wore a white toga, a sign that he had come of age. But Atia knew more about her son's state of health at that time than Caesar did, and she feared that campaigning in Africa with such a vigorous commander might be more than Octavian's frail constitution could stand.

When Caesar returned from Africa he made Octavian a member of his household and gave him a conspicuous part in the extraordinary 40-day celebration, called a "triumph," held in honor of his victories of the past 10 years. For this occasion he gave Octavian military medals, even though Octavian had never been near a battlefield, and had him ride in a chariot close behind his own. The crowds, who adored Caesar, cheered him as he rode in four consecutive grand processions, resplendent in purple and gold. Always on the lookout for celebrities among the nobility, the watchers took note — as Caesar intended they should — of the slender youth with the unruly blond hair who rode in such a prominent place of honor. There would be whispers as they found out who he was and then applause for the favored male of great Caesar's line.

Caesar was all powerful. Like Sulla, he assumed the title of dictator, but unlike Sulla, he did not intend to resign. The Senate heaped honors upon him, but he treated most of its members contemptuously, ruling by decrees for which he demanded

How far Caesar's discerning eye perceived greatness in Octavius is a matter of speculation. That Caesar was attracted by him and gave him opportunities to prove his abilities is a fact.
—HENRY THOMPSON ROWELL
American historian

A 16th-century Flemish tapestry depicts Julius Caesar in a *triumph*, the elaborate parade through Rome that was awarded to victorious generals. Although Octavian's delicate health kept him from participating in Caesar's military activities, he was given a prominent place in his granduncle's triumph as a sign of Caesar's favor.

Senate approval. He instituted many reforms and began vast public works, all overdue and necessary, but in such a high-handed manner that his upper-class colleagues were insulted and angry. If Caesar knew this, he did not care. He was impatient with the old republican form of government, feeling that it had outlived its time.

His rule was an education for Octavian. Young and impressionable, he admired his granduncle's decisiveness and efficiency. He agreed with him that there should be new roads, temples, libraries; that the marshes surrounding Rome should be drained; that the calendar should be brought up to date; that more people — even the long-haired, trousered Gauls — should be made Roman citizens. Obviously the only way to get something done in Rome was the way his granduncle did it, disregarding opposition. Octavian was not mature enough to see that Caesar might go too far in his treatment of members of his own class — nobles whose resentment increased day by day.

Always impatient and easily bored, Caesar longed to lead an army once more before he became too old. He was 56, and time was short. This time he planned a massive campaign against distant Parthia (modern Iran). He expected to leave Rome in the spring of 44 B.C. and join 6 legions — the basic infantry unit of the Roman army, each consisting of approximately 5,500 soldiers — that were stationed near Apollonia, a city in northwest Greece, across the Adriatic Sea. He planned to take his grandnephew with him on his staff as *magister equitum* (master of the horse). Since Octavian had no military training, he was sent ahead to spend the winter being drilled by commanders in the field and to complete his academic education in Apollonia's university. Caesar was to join him later after finishing up some business with the Senate on the Ides of March (March 15), 44 B.C.

> *Cowards die many times before their death. The valiant never taste of death but once.*
> —JULIUS CAESAR
> from the *Tragedy of Julius Caesar*,
> William Shakespeare

2

Heir to Caesar

Octavian never saw Julius Caesar again. At the meeting of the Roman Senate on the Ides of March, 44 B.C., a group of senators who feared Caesar's authoritarian power suddenly surrounded the dictator, drew daggers from the folds of their togas, and stabbed him to death. His most loyal friend, Mark Antony, a rugged, impulsive man, had been detained in an antechamber by one of the conspirators, who made the big mistake of letting him live.

In the confused days following Caesar's murder, Antony played a clever game. Biding his time and hiding his outrage, he invited the 60 conspirators to dinner in order to find out their strength and their future plans. The following day, using his authority as Caesar's colleague in the consulship, he called back the rest of the senators who had fled in fright and persuaded them to announce a general pardon. At the same time he went to Caesar's distraught widow, Calpurnia, and talked her into turning over to him Caesar's private papers and much

Octavius had no official status, he was the recognized head of no party; he was merely a private citizen and kinsman of the dead Caesar and . . . the intriguers at Rome did not seem to have included the possible ambitions of Octavius in their calculations.
—JOHN B. FIRTH
English historian

Mark Antony displays the bloodied toga of his friend and mentor Julius Caesar. The assassination of Caesar on the Ides of March, 44 B.C., was a turning point in Octavian's life. At the time, Octavian was unaware that Caesar had adopted him as his son, making him heir to a vast fortune and a powerful political legacy.

A senator addresses his colleagues in the Roman Senate. When Caesar declared himself dictator for life in 44 B.C., many senators became alarmed about the loss of their political power.

of his immense personal fortune. With plenty of money to pay Caesar's loyal troops and with Caesar's papers to give him authority, Antony felt sure that he soon would be in a position of supreme power.

Then he made his most successful move: He got permission from the Senate to make the oration at Caesar's funeral. Here he had sweet revenge on the cowardly assassins of his friend and leader. So inflammatory was his speech over Caesar's bloody corpse that the frenzied crowd grabbed anything that would burn, built a huge funeral pyre for their beloved commander, and headed with firebrands for the conspirators' houses. Terrified, the conspirators fled the city. Instead of achieving the restoration of the glorious Roman republic, their inglorious action had hastened its end.

Unfortunately for Antony, his funeral oration would turn out to be the high point of his career. He had ignored a few short lines in Caesar's will, added by the dictator when he was putting his affairs in order before his planned departure for Parthia. These additions were of such magnitude that they changed history.

Caesar had made the 18-year-old Octavian his heir and left him three-quarters of his fortune. Even more important, he had adopted Octavian as his son and given him his name — Gaius Julius Caesar — to which was added his grandnephew's family name in the form of Octavianus.

Octavian was no longer a distant grandnephew. To Romans an adopted son was a real son of the family. To be great Caesar's son and bear his famous name was to give Octavian an advantage that no one at the time foresaw. Antony, confident of future power and fatally miscalculating the steely character of Caesar's heir, left Rome for a month.

The horrifying news of Caesar's assassination was brought to Octavian two weeks later at his camp at Apollonia. A freedman (a freed slave) of his mother's had hurried across the sea to him with a letter in which Atia described how a group of senators led by Marcus Junius Brutus and Gaius Cassius Longinus had brutally murdered the undefended Caesar. She urged him to return to Rome at once. The freedman, who had left Rome as soon as the family heard the news, knew nothing about the political situation in the city, but he stated that any relative of Caesar's might be in danger from the powerful conspirators.

Octavian's close friend Agrippa urged him to call up the six legions that had been waiting for Caesar to lead them to Parthia and instead take them to Italy to avenge Caesar's death. He argued that the legions had been fiercely loyal to Caesar and would therefore transfer that loyalty to his favorite grandnephew. Other hotheads agreed that this was the only course to pursue.

Octavian, however, decided that it would be smarter to first find out exactly what was going on at home. Although his mind was full of hatred toward those who had murdered the man he idolized, he recognized his own inexperience and thought his best bet would be to move slowly. Taking his mother's advice, he sailed for Italy, accompanied only by Agrippa and a few others. He also took the advice of his mother's freedman and avoided the major port of Brundisium (modern Brindisi) on the Adriatic Sea, where he feared enemies might be watching for him, and instead beached his boat some 20 miles to the south of the port. Here villagers told him that the conspirators had been ignominiously scattered

Caesar and his wife, Calpurnia. Caesar was aware of the rumors of plots against his life but refused to take any precautionary measures. Legend has it that Calpurnia, frightened by a dream of Caesar's death, begged her husband not to go to the Senate on the Ides of March.

Caesar's body is carried out of the Senate by slaves. At the late dictator's funeral, Mark Antony delivered such a fiery speech against the assassins that the Roman plebs vowed vengeance. Brutus and Cassius fled Rome with their troops, thus setting the stage for civil war.

by the Roman mob after Mark Antony's stirring funeral speech. And here for the first time he learned that he had been given a large inheritance and Caesar's name.

Octavian now felt he could risk walking to Brundisium. As he hoped, the soldiers stationed in the garrison there turned out to welcome Caesar's son. He picked up another letter from his mother begging him to come directly to her country villa, and a letter from his stepfather urging him just as strongly to lie low and to turn down both his dangerous new name and his inheritance. Marcius Philippus was a cautious man, and his advice reflected his experience with Rome's deadly political factions of recent decades. He feared that Octavian's involvement would cost the youth his life.

Octavian wrote them that he meant to go to Rome to avenge his adoptive father's murder and succeed to his power. Any other 18 year old, physically delicate and without political experience, might have considered the situation hopeless. But Octavian was determined to live up to Caesar's expectations of him. That meant he had to follow in Caesar's footsteps, with Caesar's courage. At this point he was the only person in the state who thought he could succeed, but he had brains, patience, determination—and great Caesar's powerful name.

He traveled slowly toward Rome, welcomed along the way by Caesar's old veterans, who instantly responded to the magic of his name. He soon had a sizable following. As Octavian neared the city, people saw a halo around the sun, an ancient sign of royalty. Later, during public games that he gave at his own expense in memory of Caesar, a huge comet appeared and blazed in the sky for seven days. Spectators believed the comet was actually Caesar, now a star in the heavens — but Octavian believed that the star was born for him.

When Antony returned to Rome, expecting to consolidate his power, he found that young Octavian's arrival in the city had drastically changed the political climate. He discovered that he had a dangerous rival after all.

Octavian had moved in with the wisdom and sureness of an experienced politician. Not only had he treated the public to splendid games that lasted for 10 days, but he had paid Caesar's veterans the bonuses that had been promised them, insinuating that he would have paid them more if Antony had not taken so much from Caesar's widow. He had also sold some of his inherited property to fund Caesar's legacy to the more than 250,000 poor families in the city—an enormous sum, more than 3 months of each laborer's wage. He had been careful to refer to Caesar as "my father" in every speech, which endeared him to the people, as did his innocent and youthful appearance. As a mark of mourning for Caesar he let his light-colored beard grow long.

Octavian had expected that Antony, as Caesar's best friend and right-hand man, would embrace Caesar's son and work with him to avenge Caesar's murder. But Antony resented the fact that Caesar had not chosen him as heir instead of this obscure, unmilitary young relative. He kept Octavian waiting for an interview and then proved surly and hostile, refusing — since he had spent most of it — to give back the money that Caesar had left his new son in his will. This was Octavian's first bitter realization that some of the men he counted on as friends might instead turn out to be enemies. Another important man who later disappointed him was the famous orator and staunch republican Marcus Tullius Cicero, who was outwardly friendly to Octavian, but who wrote to an associate, "Let us use and praise this adolescent, and then drop him!"

Neither Antony nor Cicero understood that Octavian would be relentless in pursuing the goals he had set for himself: to avenge Caesar's murder and succeed to his power. In achieving the second of his goals, Octavian would destroy them both.

The orator and philosopher Marcus Tullius Cicero was a fervent republican and opponent of Julius Caesar's. When Octavian returned to Rome to make his own bid for power, Cicero, believing him to be naive and inexperienced, offered the youth his support, intending to use him to reestablish the republic, and then to discard him.

3

Son of a God

Fifteen months after Octavian entered Rome as the son of Caesar, he demanded to be made consul — the highest office in the Roman state. This was an outrageous demand; the legal age for the consulship was 43, and he was not yet 20. But the vacillating Senate, aware of the tremendous support for Octavian from the veterans and the people of the city, agreed to call a special election. To no one's surprise, the 19-year-old Octavian got the job. As consul, he now could negotiate with Antony, a former consul, from a position of equal power and prestige.

Antony could no longer ignore this upstart who, he bitterly remarked, owed everything to Caesar's name. In the early winter of 43 B.C., he arranged a secret, heavily guarded meeting with Octavian and a third man, Marcus Aemilius Lepidus, Antony's colleague, who had also served under Caesar. At the end of two days the three men had struck some

Mark Antony's rival was a youth of 20, frail and inexperienced except for the bitter struggle of the past year, but possessed of a tenacity of purpose and a grasp of the means of attaining his ends that are perhaps unparalleled in the history of youth.
—LILY ROSS TAYLOR
historian

At the Egyptian court, Cleopatra receives Mark Antony in her throne room. Antony, an experienced general and politician, was expected to succeed Caesar, but Octavian cleverly used Antony's involvement with Cleopatra, whom the Romans distrusted, to arouse opposition against his powerful rival.

Queen Cleopatra is depicted on a relief from Thebes, Egypt. Cleopatra ruled Egypt as a Roman client kingdom. She retained independence of government in her own realm but owed the Romans aid, in the form of money or troops, if military necessity demanded it.

cynical bargains. Using as their model the powerful First Triumvirate of Caesar, Pompey, and Crassus, they agreed to form the Second Triumvirate for the purpose of "ordering the republic" — a euphemism for seizing absolute control for five years.

Then they faced up to the problem of money. They were badly in need of funds. The two chief conspirators, Brutus and Cassius, had fled with 20 legions to Greece and were receiving tribute from the wealthy eastern provinces — tribute that ordinarily would have gone to Rome. An overseas campaign against them would be very expensive.

Antony and Lepidus suggested a sure way of raising money, used effectively some years back by the dictator Sulla: the proscription of enemies and minor officials who happened to be rich. The lives of the proscribed men would be forfeit and their property confiscated. Besides providing funds for an expeditionary force, the proscription would insure that no friends of Caesar's assassins would be left in Italy to make mischief while the triumvirs were out of the country.

Octavian at first protested, but the others pointed out what had happened to Caesar when he let too many of his enemies survive. Because Octavian's first goal was to destroy Caesar's murderers, he overcame any scruples he may have had and became as calculating a terrorist as his two partners.

The proscription lists were made public the very night that Octavian, Antony, and Lepidus were formally elected triumvirs. Three hundred senators and 2,000 rich businessmen were named for execution. Most of them had time to flee the country, leaving their riches behind, but many did not escape the bloodbath. One of the victims was Cicero, the preeminent defender of the dying republic, who had dared to criticize both Antony and Octavian. He was seized and beheaded by Antony's soldiers, who brought his head and hands back to Rome and nailed them to the speaker's stand in the Forum, the scene of many of Cicero's most stirring orations. Antony's wife, Fulvia, coming to gloat over the head of her husband's old enemy, pierced his once dangerous tongue with a jeweled pin. As historian Chester G. Starr wrote, "No act could better have symbolized the complete end of the Roman Republic."

The reconciliation of Antony and Octavian was strengthened, at least on the surface, by ties of kinship when a marriage was arranged between Octavian and Claudia, the very young daughter of Fulvia. Gossips of the time said that this was a marriage in name only, because Octavian detested his malicious mother-in-law and was not inclined to love her daughter. In any case, the marriage, having achieved its immediate political purpose of calming relations between Octavian and Antony, soon ended in divorce.

In January 42 B.C. the Senate formally made the late dictator Julius Caesar a god. Now Octavian could — and did — call himself "Son of the Divine Caesar." This gave him another big political advantage. All Romans revered many gods and would extend that reverence to a god's son.

In the fall of that year, Antony and Octavian took some 20 legions of Caesar's loyal veterans to Philippi in northeastern Greece, where an equal number of legions, led by Brutus and Cassius, awaited them. This was warfare on a huge scale — almost a quarter of a million men — but weighted in favor of the attackers by the poor communications and disorganization of the conspirators' armies. In addition, there was a leadership problem because Brutus was haunted by dreams of Caesar's ghost and overwhelmed by a sense of doom. According to the poet Horace, who as a young Roman soldier took part in the fight, the conspirators' troops lost courage, threw their shields away, and groveled, their chins in the dust. At the end, both Brutus and Cassius committed suicide and most of the other conspirators died in battle. With their deaths went the last chance of restoring the Roman republic.

Octavian, suffering one of his recurring bouts of sickness, won no glory at Philippi. Rumors spread that he spent the first battle in his tent and part of the second one hiding in a marsh when his tent was

In 43 B.C. Octavian and Antony agreed to form a coalition to rule Rome. The third member of the Second Triumvirate was Marcus Aemilius Lepidus, the governor of Transalpine Gaul and a supporter of Antony's.

Fearing they might find their own names, senators read a list of declared state enemies. As a means of gaining immediate cash, the Second Triumvirate followed the example of the 1st-century B.C. military dictator Lucius Cornelius Sulla, who posted proscription lists of enemies and confiscated their property.

about to be overrun. As he later explained (or excused) himself in his autobiography, he had left his headquarters on the orders of his doctor, who had had a dream warning of disaster. It is certainly conceivable that the doctor took one look at his feverish and prostrate patient and used the device of a dream to save him. In ancient times prophetic dreams were taken very seriously. It is also conceivable that his comrade-in-arms Agrippa had him carried unconscious in a litter to a safe place, because it would have been disastrous to the army's morale for him to be killed by the conspirators. It is also quite possible that Octavian, physically weak during all of his youth and now even weaker from sickness, feared with good reason that if he fought man-to-man against tough legionaries, his planned career would end abruptly.

In any case, Antony saw to it that his friends in Rome heard the malicious rumors about Octavian's inglorious conduct in battle. Only the name of his father, Caesar the god, kept the veterans loyal to him and saved Octavian from disgrace.

Caesar's assassins were now dead, and their revolting deed of two years past had been avenged. Many years later, when time and success had softened the memories of the battle at Philippi, Octavian, then emperor, published a description of his role in it: "I drove into exile the men who butchered my parent, avenging their crime; and afterwards, when they made war on the Republic, I twice de-

One victim of the Second Triumvirate's proscription was Cicero, who had begun to criticize the triumvirs for their failure to restore the republic. Antony's wife, Fulvia, ordered Cicero's head brought to her so she could pierce with a pin the tongue that had delivered so many fiery speeches against her husband.

When it became apparent that he had lost the Battle of Philippi, Brutus committed suicide. Soon afterward, Cassius also killed himself, and so died the last of those who tried to restore the Roman republic.

feated them in pitched battle." By then he had no need to mention the name of Mark Antony, who by his excellent generalship had been the real victor at Philippi. But right after the battle both men knew the true story.

The victors divided Rome's empire between them. Antony picked by far the richest half — the civilized provinces of the east, among them Egypt, Syria, Asia Minor, and Greece. He assigned Octavian the troubled western half, which included Italy, Gaul, and Spain. He hoped that the responsibility for curing the problems of the West would prove too much for Octavian and ruin whatever reputation he had left after his recent cowardly behavior. Lepidus, the third member of the Triumvirate, could be almost ignored because he had not been at the fight and had lost all influence on the legions. He was eventually given the governorship of the small province of Africa (modern Tunisia), far out of the political mainstream.

Antony, heady with success, took the greater part of the army and made an almost royal procession through the Roman provinces in Asia Minor (the western part of modern Turkey), exacting tribute from inland monarchs and money from the Roman coastal towns. At one of these towns, the bewitching queen of Egypt, Cleopatra, sailed in a golden barge to meet the Roman general. Antony was fascinated by her at first sight, as Julius Caesar had been six years earlier. Like Caesar, who had lived with Cleopatra for a while in Egypt and had a son by her, Antony accepted her invitation to spend the winter at her court in the Egyptian city of Alexandria.

Octavian's progress was not as glamorous as Antony's. He was so ill that he barely made it home to Italy. Rumors of his death preceded him. When he finally arrived, his face ashen and his slim body skin and bones, most people believed — and some hoped —that the problems of Rome would finish him off.

In 42 B.C. Quintus Horatius Flaccus (known as Horace) was a young soldier in Brutus's army at Philippi. Later, as a renowned poet, Horace recounted how Brutus's own sense of doom led his men to lose courage and surrender to Antony and Octavian.

4

Taking Control

When Octavian returned to the shores of Italy in the fall of 42 B.C. he was just 21 and only beginning to recover from his debilitating illness. Though his body had weakened, his resolve had hardened. Determined to put his personal disaster at Philippi behind him, he coolly assessed his chances.

He had his legions, who still looked with affection upon the son of Caesar. He had his loyal boyhood friend Agrippa, who had fought well at Philippi and was turning out to be an excellent field commander. He had an equally loyal adviser, Gaius Maecenas, a wealthy businessman who was adept at working behind the scenes on his behalf. Octavian knew many well-placed people in Rome who were ready to support him if he managed his strategy well. And he was, after all, a triumvir of Rome, the legal possessor of immense, though shared, power.

But the problems that confronted him were enormous. Law and order had broken down. A few old-style Roman generals, remnants of the faction that had distrusted Caesar, were moving small armies

It cannot be denied that as a young man he was ruthless and unscrupulous. It can be urged in his excuse that he was in a very vulnerable position, and that his adversaries were also unscrupulous and ruthless.
—A. H. M. JONES
English historian

General and politician Marcus Vipsanius Agrippa was a boyhood friend of Octavian's. The success of Octavian's bid for political control of Rome was due in large part to Agrippa's military genius, and the general, until his death, continued to serve Augustus loyally.

Augustus holds an audience at the Forum. In the early part of his reign, Augustus encouraged Roman citizens to come to his house on the Palatine, where he would listen to their petitions.

unchecked through northern Italy. In the south the powerful general Sextus Pompey, son of the Pompey who had been Julius Caesar's enemy, controlled Sicily. His pirate navy intercepted the big grain ships on which the hungry urban poor in Rome depended, causing famine and rioting in Rome. Other ambitious generals in the provinces of Gaul and Spain were preparing to swoop upon Italy the moment Octavian faltered. The veterans who had returned with him from Philippi demanded the land that had been promised them, but rich landowners rushed to Rome to oppose the grants and successfully lobbied corruptible senators, many of whom were Antony's friends working behind the scenes for Octavian's downfall.

But Octavian's assignment to the western half of the Roman Empire, far from finishing him off as Antony had intended, turned out to be his great opportunity. He may not have had physical courage in battle, but he had another kind of courage. As he moved coolly and skillfully from one dangerous situation to another, people of all classes gradually came to realize that in addition to Caesar's name, he had Caesar's iron determination. Instead of drawing ridicule, his frail physique and quiet, almost academic manner became assets, attracting followers who were sick of the contentious and arrogant political leaders of the recent past.

Octavian placated the landowners with deals and promises while breaking up their large estates into countless small farms, thereby making farmers out of 100,000 veterans and creating an important new rural population throughout Italy. Then he tried to win the formidable Sextus Pompey over to his side by marrying one of Sextus's relatives, a twice-married, older woman named Scribonia — young enough, however, to bear two years later Octavian's only child, his much-loved daughter Julia, who later broke his heart. Octavian's second politically arranged marriage proved no more successful than his first one, but it did postpone for a while his inevitable confrontation with Sextus.

Meanwhile there remained in the north of Italy the ambitious, conspiring generals with their personal armies, dangerous threats that would have to be met. In the fall of 41 B.C. Octavian gave Agrippa his first command, ordering him to destroy these armies. By the end of the summer the rebels had retreated into the hill town of Perusia (Perugia), 85 miles north of Rome, which they believed to be impregnable. Here Octavian joined Agrippa for part of a bitter winter's siege. By spring the starving town surrendered. Its leading citizens, former members of the party that had long plotted against Caesar, now stood before Caesar's son and begged for their lives.

But the years when Octavian could afford to be merciful lay far in the future. He had learned the propaganda value of ruthlessness and terror and needed to give a frightening example to any other town that might be considering rebellion. He spared only one man who had once voted publicly to condemn Caesar's murderers. To the rest of the 300 senators, businessmen, and town councillors who asked for mercy he coldly answered, "You must die!"

On the day Octavian's divorce from Scribonia became official, she gave birth to their daughter. The girl, named Julia, would be Octavian's only natural child.

He and Agrippa then marched the army north to Gaul, where the Roman commander — under Octavian's rule according to the arrangement made with Antony — was treasonously working against him. He removed the general, turned over control of the 11 legions stationed there to a more trustworthy commander, and returned to Rome. He was now, through his own strategy and Agrippa's skill, master of Gaul and Italy.

During the winter that Perusia was starving, Antony was luxuriating in the warm, dry land of Egypt with his mistress, Cleopatra. Antony was a strange mixture of personalities — at one moment full of energy, the next moment idle and self-indulgent. He had received no news from Italy because during the stormy winter months the Mediterranean Sea was too dangerous for sailing ships, with their awkward rigging, and for the shallower ships rowed by slaves. When the sea lanes reopened in the spring of 40 B.C. he heard for the first time the news of Octavian's successes in Perusia and Gaul. Suspicious and fu-

Cleopatra entertains Antony at dinner in this 16th-century Italian painting. While Octavian was consolidating his power over the western half of Roman territory, Antony was immersing himself in the grandeur of the Egyptian court and increasingly alienating his fellow Romans.

rious, he returned to Italy to confront his young colleague. For a while there was a chance of a battle between them, but their soldiers, many of whom were old comrades, refused to fight each other. The two men met at the port of Brundisium, where Octavian was able to convince the older man of his good intentions, and they patched up their shaky alliance.

The triumvirate was renewed for another five years and the old distribution of power was confirmed: Octavian controlled Italy, Dalmatia (the coast of modern Yugoslavia), Spain, and Gaul; Antony was in charge of all the eastern provinces from Greece to the Euphrates River; Lepidus, the unimportant third member, remained in charge of the small province of Africa. The triumvirs paid a visit to Rome, where an ovation was held, but it was marred by the boos and stone-throwing of the city mob, which was being slowly starved by Sextus's blockade of the grain supply. For the moment the three had to concede Sicily to the piratical Sextus, going so far as to promise him a consulship if he would let the grain ships through. But Sextus was a vain, ambitious man who had hoped that the triumvirs would ask him to join them as rulers of the empire. He continued to interfere with Rome's food supply and would have to be dealt with sooner or later.

Now it was Antony's turn to make a political marriage. His wife Fulvia had recently died and he was hundreds of miles away from the intoxicating influence of Cleopatra. When it was proposed that he marry Octavian's favorite sister, Octavia, a beautiful young widow with three children, he agreed.

This tie of blood reassured many, particularly the soldiers who had worried about a fight to the death between Caesar's old friend and Caesar's son. Others, less naive, were sure that such a fight was merely postponed. And those who knew Antony well felt that his tastes were too flamboyant to be satisfied for long with his quiet and well-bred young wife. They feared that he would desert her, a provocation that her brother would not ignore.

Octavian's youngest sister, Octavia, became an unfortunate pawn in her brother's political schemes. Octavian arranged for her to marry Antony, who hoped to cement an alliance with his fellow triumvir and thus prevent the growing estrangement between them from becoming an open rift.

This model of a Roman war barge was constructed in 19th-century France. In order to destroy the pirate fleet of Sextus Pompey, who was preventing grain deliveries from reaching Rome, Octavian ordered an intensive shipbuilding program to begin and appointed Agrippa commander of the fleet.

Antony returned to the east in 39 B.C., taking his new wife Octavia to Greece with him. Octavian went in the other direction — to Gaul, where he installed Agrippa as governor, an important career step for the general on the Roman ladder of honor.

Octavian then prepared for an all-out war against Sextus in Sicily. Without a navy he could not hope to destroy the pirate's devastating blockades, so he started a shipbuilding program from scratch and trained hundreds of slaves to be oarsmen. They practiced speedy maneuvers on a shallow inland lake that had been connected to the open sea by a canal.

Meanwhile Octavian divorced Scribonia, saying that he could not bear the way she nagged at him. The divorce served also as a convenient political announcement of a real break with Sextus, now that their hypocritical family relationship was ended. But the real truth was that for the first time in his life, Octavian had fallen passionately in love.

Livia Drusilla was a member of one of Rome's most ancient noble families — a group that had been aloof toward Octavian. When he first met her, she was the young wife of an equally well-born aristocrat, Tiberius Claudius Nero. She was a delicately beautiful brunette with large eyes and a small, fine nose and mouth. She had a two-year-old son, Tiberius, and was some months into her second pregnancy.

After their first meeting, Octavian immediately shaved off his beard to improve his appearance — a sign of real interest, for he was generally careless about grooming. Whether this was the step that first won her attention will never be known, but she too fell in love, left her husband, and moved in with him. Livia's husband granted her a divorce, and Octavian's divorce went through on the very day that Scribonia gave birth to his daughter, Julia.

In 38 B.C. Octavian married Livia Drusilla, a member of one of Rome's most distinguished aristocratic families. Although the marriage was a brilliant political move that ensured the support of Rome's aristocracy, Octavian apparently truly loved Livia, who divorced her husband to marry him.

Tiberius Claudius Nero was Livia Drusilla's eldest son by her first husband. He was two years old when Livia left her husband for Octavian, an event that would change the course of Tiberius's life.

Octavian immediately obtained special permission from the state priests to marry Livia while she was pregnant by her first husband.

When Octavian and Livia were married in 38 B.C., he was 25 and she was 19. Their marriage was a love match — one of the successful marriages of history, despite their failure to produce a much-desired heir — and was ended only by his death 52 years later. Livia brought him warmth and inner security. During their long life together he loved and respected her, asking her advice on many important matters of state. She in turn was loyal and helpful to him, behaving with dignity and avoiding publicity.

Their marriage also proved to be a brilliant move for his career. Up to now Octavian's inner circle — men such as his great general Agrippa and his wise adviser Maecenas — were of obscure birth. They were of vital help to Octavian, but to be successful in Rome he also needed the backing of the old aristocratic families, who so far had stayed snobbishly on the sidelines. Now, through his marriage to Livia, the aristocrats considered him one of their class and flocked to support him. Octavian became more relaxed. He still had bouts of sudden sickness, but he no longer suffered the chronic ill health that had crippled his adolescence. His confidence grew; his shy and distant personality warmed up. Although he had no public opinion polls to consult, he knew that all the important groups in Italy — the legions, the city crowds, the businessmen, and the nobles — would stand solidly behind him when he faced, one after the other, the two men who stood between him and supremacy.

In viewing the married life of Augustus and Livia . . . an American may well think of George and Martha Washington; of all modern historical characters the Father of our Country perhaps approaches most clearly the symbolic, statuesque dignity and respectability of the Pater Patriae.
—CHESTER G. STARR
American historian

5
Antony's Challenge

Antony meanwhile had done nothing to match Octavian's consolidation of power. He had spent most of the past three years in Athens, using it as headquarters for administering Rome's eastern provinces. Octavia had borne him a daughter and was dutifully bringing up his three children by his first wife, Fulvia. This houseful of children and respectable domesticity began to bore him, as did Octavia's goodness and modesty. He longed for more action.

In the back of his mind he had always shared Caesar's ambition to conquer Parthia, the huge country that so far had resisted Rome's grasp. The possibilities intrigued him. A military conquest of Parthia would not only bring glory to Rome but would make him once more a popular military hero. He would be granted a Roman triumph comparable to Caesar's, riding to the applause of the people behind thousands of chained, exotic captives and festive wagonloads of treasure, while his co-triumvir Octavian, a notoriously incompetent soldier, would fade into the obscurity he deserved.

There could not be two masters of the Empire with irreconcilable temperaments and divergent purposes.
—JOHN BUCHAN
on the struggle for power between Augustus and Antony

By the end of the fourth decade B.C., Octavian was ready to challenge Antony for supreme control of Rome. Using the Romans' suspicion and dislike of Cleopatra, Octavian conducted a clever propaganda campaign against Antony in order to erode his rival's support in the city.

But a campaign against Parthia would demand more troops and money than he had. He knew of only one person — Cleopatra of Egypt — who had the fortune to support his plan. He had not seen her for almost four years, but the thought of her money and the memory of her charms proved irresistible. In 37 B.C. he sent the pregnant Octavia back to Rome — a deliberate insult to her brother. Then he left Greece and rejoined Cleopatra in Egypt.

They became lovers once more. He was now 46, still handsome in a coarse and rugged way. She was 32, more intriguing than ever, ambitious as he — and cleverer. Her goal was to recreate the great eastern empire of her ancestors, the Ptolemies, and she intended to use Antony to achieve it. She encouraged her lover's weakness for pomp and luxury. Soon he was behaving like an Oriental monarch, wearing embroidered Egyptian robes, living in un-

A Roman general celebrates a victory with a triumph. The vision of military glory led Antony to attempt to conquer Parthia in 36 B.C. A vast, powerful empire situated on the eastern border of the Roman provinces, Parthia had long been desired by the Romans.

paralleled luxury, flattered and even worshiped by the multitude as the Egyptian god Osiris. Cleopatra easily persuaded him to acknowledge publicly their three-year-old twin son and daughter. Doted upon by this bewitching woman, Antony soon was promising considerable eastern territories to her and to their children. In exchange she gave him the money, supplies, and ships he needed for his Parthian expedition. In the spring of 36 B.C. he set out for Parthia at the head of 60,000 legionaries, 10,000 horsemen from Gaul and Spain, and 30,000 soldiers from Rome's eastern allies.

That same year Octavian began an offensive against Sextus in Sicily. His plan was sound: Agrippa was to command the newly built navy and attack the island on one side while the triumvir Lepidus was to cross over from Africa and invade the island from the south. Octavian would land his

A reconstruction of the *Ara Pacis*, or Altar of Peace — a monument that depicted the leading figures of the Augustan Age in a religious procession. As early as his defeat of Sextus Pompey, Octavian was seen as a bringer of peace and stability to Rome.

legions on a third side. He hoped to restore some kind of military glory to his name, but he soon ran into difficulties. Violent storms destroyed half of his squadron and shipwrecked him. On shore he was surrounded by enemy cavalry and barely escaped. For the only time in his life he thought of suicide and begged a friend to kill him with his sword.

The other commanders, however, accomplished their part of the plan. Agrippa's fast war galleys with their trained slave rowers and fighting marines rushed at Sextus's ships, lowered their massive grappling irons onto the enemy decks, and soon sent Sextus's men to the bottom of the sea. Lepidus successfully landed his legions from Africa on the Sicilian shore. Sextus escaped to the east where, captured by Roman troops the following year, he met his death.

Octavian joined Agrippa for the rest of the campaign, which was simply a mopping-up operation — with one extraordinary note. Lepidus, having brooded for years over his humiliating treatment by Antony and Octavian, thought he saw his chance to get even. Now that his own 14 legions had been augmented by the surrendered legions of Sextus, he dared to send an impudent message to Octavian — who had far fewer men — demanding Sicily in addition to his assigned province of Africa. But Lepidus had seriously miscalculated Octavian's character and his ability to win the hearts of men. Octavian had not spent all this time and agony reconquering Sicily merely to hand it over to a man he despised. With only a few attendants he walked into Lepidus's camp and made a speech to the soldiers, who thronged around him. His bravery in coming unarmed among them, his slim, boyish appearance, and his quiet authority won them over, and they deserted, cheering, to his side. It was a brilliant performance.

Lepidus threw himself abjectly at Octavian's feet, expecting the worst, but Octavian took this opportunity to demonstrate to his countrymen that the days of vengeful proscriptions and executions were over. He took over Lepidus's province of Africa, but allowed the foolish man to live in powerless retirement. He was not so kind to the escaped slaves who had made up a large part of Sextus's army. Without

Roman soldiers stand aboard a *bireme*, or galley with two tiers of oars on each side. Using such vessels in 36 B.C., Octavian launched his offensive against Sextus Pompey. Under Agrippa's skillful command, Octavian's forces destroyed the pirate fleet, and Octavian's control of the western part of Rome's holdings was complete.

A statue of Augustus stands outside Agrippa's palace in Rome. Augustus's closest adviser, Agrippa was an integral part of the emperor's construction program in the capital. He built an enormous public bath that became the model after which later baths were designed.

misgivings he followed the traditional Roman practice: He returned many slaves to their Italian masters for punishment and crucified the rest — some 6,000 men.

His homecoming was celebrated with wild enthusiasm. Not only had he restored Sicily to Rome's control, but he had ended the famine caused by Sextus's blockade; the big lumbering grain ships were once more unloading African and Sicilian wheat at Italian ports. Senators and citizens flocked to greet him and escort him to his house and to the temples. In gratitude they heaped honors upon him, erecting triumphal arches and installing statues of him in the temples in Rome and throughout the West. The day of Sextus's defeat was made into an annual holiday. Like Caesar, Octavian was granted the right to wear a laurel wreath on all public occasions — but unlike Caesar, honors meant little to him and he refused as many as he tactfully could. He was proud, however, of the inscription carved on the base of a gilded column in the Forum, declaring that he had reestablished the peace so long disturbed on land and sea. Though this would not be fully realized as long as his rival Antony was alive, it was the first public acknowledgment of the Augustan Peace (Pax Augusta) for which he would become renowned throughout history.

During the celebrations Octavian also acknowledged Agrippa's military genius. With great ceremony he awarded Agrippa an extraordinary crown decorated with miniature "beaks" — the iron points on the prows of warships — to wear on state occasions.

Octavian knew that now or never he would have to achieve some success in actual combat on the battlefield. Rome had always been a military state, ruled by men who at some point in their lives had led legions into action, and Romans in their heart of hearts were impressed by brute courage. Octavian's opportunity came in the frontier province of Illyricum (part of modern Yugoslavia). This province consisted mostly of a strategic coastal road carrying the important traffic running east and west: horsemen, troops, traders with their loaded bullock wagons, even tourists. This road was becoming increasingly threatened by wild tribes from the interior mountain country. It had to be kept open, and the northern frontier had to be secured. In a short campaign that he organized and commanded, Octavian forced himself to risk his life in the thick of the fighting. Of course he was heavily guarded, but a stone from a sling hit him, and a bridge collapsed under him, giving him the "honorable wounds" that every Roman sought. Although he had been called *imperator*, or victorious general, before this campaign, at last he felt that he had earned the title. In a few generations this title came to mean "emperor."

He [Augustus] always felt horrified and insulted when called "My Lord," a form of address used by slaves to their owners.
—SUETONIUS
Roman historian

Antony and Cleopatra appear in a ceremony dressed as the Egyptian deities Osiris and Isis. In 34 B.C. Romans were shocked to learn that Antony, who had married Cleopatra two years earlier, had given her and their children lands in the East that rightfully belonged to Rome.

While Octavian was bringing stability to the West, Antony was bungling his job of conquest in the East. His massive Parthian expedition proved a miserable failure, forcing him to retreat and to lose thousands of his most experienced soldiers. Although he sent word to Rome that he had won a great victory, other messengers brought a different story. Octavian saw to it that the news of Antony's fiasco was widely publicized.

Antony further played into Octavian's hands by marrying Cleopatra while he was still married to

Octavia. In Egypt it was customary for a ruler to have as many wives as he pleased, but in conservative Rome it was not only shocking but illegal. Romans sided with the wronged Octavia, whose presence in Rome, tending Antony's home and loyally bringing up his children, was a constant reminder of Antony's un-Roman behavior and a daily affront to her brother, Octavian.

In 34 B.C. Antony attacked Armenia in revenge for its reneging on promised support of his Parthian campaign. Romans were astonished to learn that Antony celebrated his victory over the Armenians with a triumph in Alexandria in which Cleopatra, costumed as the Egyptian goddess Isis and seated on a golden throne, received the Armenian captives. This was the height of sacrilege. Triumphs could be celebrated only in Rome, and only the greatest Roman god, Jupiter, was supposed to receive captives, brought to his shining temple on the steep Capitoline hill.

Romans were also shocked to learn that Antony had given Cleopatra the title of Queen of Queens and made Caesarion, her 13-year-old son by Julius Caesar, King of Kings, granting them both the absolute rule of Egypt and Cyprus. At the same time Antony had bequeathed land to the children born to him and Cleopatra. Their daughter, Cleopatra Selene, was made head of the Roman province of Cyrenaica (modern Libya); her twin brother, Alexander Helios, was made king of Armenia and the land of the Medes (northwest Iran). To their other son, Ptolemy Philadelphus, Antony gave three coastal provinces. All of these grants were Roman provinces or client kingdoms. Antony had no authority to give them away without the approval of his co-ruler Octavian, the consuls, and the Roman Senate.

Antony's final insult was a more personal one. He proclaimed that Caesarion, Caesar's son, was Caesar's legitimate heir — a direct challenge to Octavian and one that he could not ignore.

> *Her actual beauty, it is said, was not in itself so remarkable that none could be compared with her . . . but the contact of her presence, if you lived with her, was irresistible.*
> —PLUTARCH
> Roman historian,
> on Cleopatra's influence
> over men

6

Master of Rome

It was now easy for Octavian to steer the Roman people toward war. His propagandists portrayed Cleopatra as an eastern sorceress who had made a traitor of a famous Roman general, and they contrasted Octavian's noble and patriotic behavior with Antony's depravity. Octavian followed this up by illegally snatching Antony's will from its safekeeping in the temple of the sacred Vestal Virgins. Waving it at the crowd, he revealed in a scathing speech Antony's scandalous bequests of Roman territory to Cleopatra and her family. Though some may have thought it was in bad taste to read a man's will while he was still alive, its shocking contents stifled all protests.

In another masterful political stroke, Octavian arranged to have all the western provinces swear an oath of allegiance to him. The second five-year term of the triumvirate had expired at the end of 33 B.C., and neither he nor Antony held an official position. This oath, however, gave Octavian the force and prestige he needed to pronounce Antony unfit to

Octavian accused Antony of every immorality, of throwing away Rome's welfare for the eastern harlot queen, of adopting eastern religion and customs . . . every appeal was made to Roman xenophobia and fears of the east to break down Antony's heroic reputation.
—ELEANOR G. HUZAR
American historian

Cleopatra commits suicide by subjecting herself to the bite of an asp. Roman history might have taken a very different turn had Cleopatra's influence over Antony not been so strong. By adopting Cleopatra's luxurious imperial life-style, Antony lost his support in Rome.

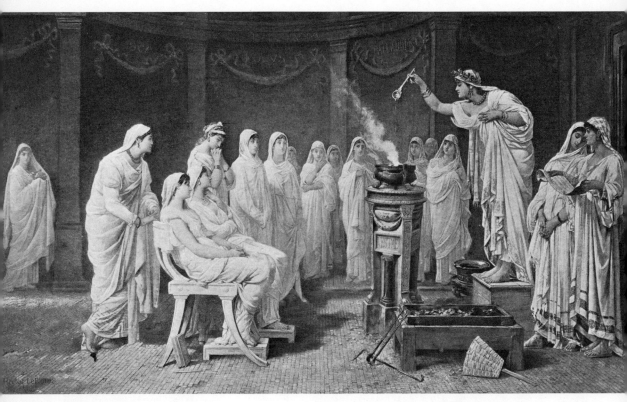

Young Roman women become members of the Vestal Virgins. The Vestals performed many sacred duties, one of which was the safekeeping of wills. Octavian illegally took Antony's will from the Vestals in order to reveal his rival's scandalous donations to Cleopatra.

rule the Roman east. The Roman people now stood behind Octavian in his role as champion of the old Roman ways.

Too late, Antony realized that he had been outwitted. In spite of more than 10 years of dealing with Octavian, he seemed never to grasp the possibility that the Roman people could actually prefer a nonmilitary man still in his twenties to a seasoned Roman general in the prime of life.

Antony now was forced to adopt a desperate strategy. He could not consider a surprise attack on the homeland of Italy as long as he had Cleopatra by his side, for the whole country would oppose him. His alternative was to cross to Greece, establish a strong base there, and force Octavian to invade. Equipping 400 heavy warships and collecting his 19 Roman legions (more than 60,000 men) and some 80,000 Asiatic auxiliaries, he crossed in the late fall of 32 B.C. to the southwestern coast of Greece. Cleopatra and her fleet of 60 ships accompanied him. As a final break with Rome, Antony sent notice of a formal divorce to Octavia.

With solemn rites Octavian declared war against the foreign invader Cleopatra, thus cleverly disguising the conflict's true nature: a civil war against Antony. Italy supported Octavian's suddenly increased military budget by paying huge taxes: Citizens, for example, had to pay one-fourth of their income; freedmen had to turn over one-eighth. Octavian left Maecenas in charge in Rome and together with Agrippa, who commanded the fleet, crossed the Adriatic Sea to Greece, landing unopposed on a point of land across from Antony's army. Octavian had a fleet slightly smaller than Antony's and had considerably fewer foot soldiers. On this showdown depended the future of the empire and the mastery of the Roman world.

Antony's cavalry and troops were a mixed, quarrelsome group: Egyptians, Judeans, Greeks, Syrians, Libyans, Arabians, and, of course, his own trained Roman legions. But the Roman legions and their commanders had been spoiled by the lazy pace of the East and lacked the fervent patriotism that

Roman cavalrymen were the original *equites*, or members of the equestrian class. By Octavian's time, however, the equestrian class was made up of wealthy businessmen who gained admission by meeting a set property qualification.

The conflict between Octavian and Antony eventually exploded at the Battle of Actium, off the west coast of Greece, in September 31 B.C. The outcome of this naval battle determined the future of Rome.

gripped their western comrades-in-arms. Even the Roman advisers who had remained loyal to Antony were squabbling among themselves. Embarrassed by Cleopatra's presence, they urged Antony to send her home, but because he was heavily dependent on the cash and supplies carried by her ships, he refused. Disease from the unsanitary conditions of the marshy coastal land added to Antony's problems.

Octavian, on the other hand, had a loyal, compact army. His legionaries were the best fighting men in the world, and they were convinced that they were defending their homeland against a foreign queen and her strange gods. Their general, Agrippa, fresh from his victories in the Sicilian war, was the best commander of the day. He proceeded to outguess and outmaneuver Antony.

Throughout the hot summer months of 31 B.C. the two armies skirmished along the craggy coast while Agrippa's navy sank the Egyptian food convoys and set up a naval blockade to prevent any more rations from getting through to Antony's troops. Already weakened from malaria, they began to desert. On the insistence of Cleopatra and against the advice of his aides, Antony decided to force the issue at sea near the promontory of Actium on the western coast of Greece.

On September 2, a windless morning, the war galleys of Octavian and Agrippa put out to sea, then rested their oars in the morning's calm waters, awaiting the enemy. In the early afternoon Antony's fleet rowed at full speed out of the harbor. Usually during sea battles commanders left their bulky rolled-up sails on shore, but Antony stored his sails on board, a sign that if he should lose the battle, he was counting on the usual fresh afternoon winds to help him escape under sail.

The hot summer sun blazed as both fleets raced toward each other, churning up the water for several miles across the mouth of the wide harbor. The hulls of many ships were reinforced with bronze and iron, and each of their long heavy oars was pulled by three, four, or possibly five men. The bigger ships on both sides carried turrets for archers and catapults; before they closed in combat they hurled rocks, arrows, and flaming missiles at each other.

Octavian commanded one wing while Agrippa took the center, facing Antony. Cleopatra's squadrons, including her treasure ships, stayed in the background throughout the day. By late afternoon the fight was going badly for Antony, with many of his ships sunk or in flames. Suddenly Cleopatra's 60 ships hoisted their sails, picked up the winds, and fled into the open sea toward Egypt.

Antony left his large flagship and boarded a speedier galley that caught up with her. When he came aboard, according to the late 1st-century Greek historian Plutarch, "He went forward by himself and sat alone, without a word, in the ship's prow, covering his face with his two hands."

Their sails soon disappeared below the horizon. When the rest of Antony's fleet saw their commander desert his post to join the Egyptian queen, their resistance broke. They surrendered to Octavian, as did Antony's armies, left leaderless in Greece.

The sea battle of Actium determined the shape of the Roman Empire for the next 500 years. Historians agree that if Octavian had lost, the eastern and western portions of the empire would gradually have separated and then degenerated into small rival states.

> *Octavian's objective was to capture Cleopatra alive to display in his triumph and to secure Antonius' death without being responsible for it.*
> —A. H. M. JONES
> English historian

By the summer of 30 B.C., Octavian had pursued Antony, who had lost the Battle of Actium, to Egypt. Unwilling to be captured by his former fellow triumvir, Antony took the action considered most noble for a defeated Roman soldier: He committed suicide.

Octavian slowly traveled down the coast of Asia Minor and Syria, accumulating tribute from the Roman coastal towns and accepting the allegiance of the kings who were all too ready to break the alliances they had made with Antony. By the summer of 30 B.C. he was closing in on Alexandria in Egypt. Depressed and hopeless, Antony committed suicide, followed shortly by Cleopatra, who did not want to be paraded in ignominy in a Roman triumph. Octavian had her son by Julius Caesar put to death, for, as the boy's disloyal teacher advised, "too many Caesars are not a good thing." He also put to death Antony's designated heir and successor, his eldest son Antyllus by his first wife Fulvia.

These were Octavian's last acts of political brutality, but at that point in his career, before he had time to consolidate the power he had sought so single-mindedly, he wanted no possible claimants left alive to challenge him. He spared Antony's other children, sending them back to Rome to be brought up by the forgiving Octavia.

A guide escorted Octavian to the tomb of Alexander the Great, the 4th-century B.C. Greek conqueror who had conquered and ruled a huge empire before his death at the age of 33. As he looked down at Alexander's mummified body, Octavian must have reflected that he had been two years younger than Alexander — and without the army that Alexander inherited — when he started out on his career. Now he was master of 60 legions, 900 warships, and all the Roman world. His task in the future was to fulfill his promise to ensure a time of peace and prosperity for the Roman people. But how would he achieve this goal?

In 30 B.C., Octavian visits the tomb of the famed 4th-century B.C. Greek conqueror Alexander the Great. Just as Alexander had conquered a vast empire by the age of 33, Octavian now ruled a huge state that included most of the Mediterranean world.

7

First Citizen

Octavian now was in complete charge of the huge Roman Empire, bounded by the Atlantic Ocean and the English Channel, by the forests of the Germans to the north, the deserts of Africa to the south, and the warlike Parthians to the east. Within these thousands of miles of frontier was an enormous diversity of races, nations, and tribes that depended entirely on one man, not yet 33 years old, who was not in the best of health and was exhausted by 14 years of strain and danger.

Before making the long trip back from Egypt to Rome, Octavian canceled all of Antony's foolish gifts of territory to Cleopatra's children. He then transformed Egypt from Cleopatra's kingdom to a Roman province — but decided to keep control of its revenues in his own hands. He had seen the vast extent of Egypt's wealth: grain from the Nile flood lands; papyrus and fine linen; quarries of colored marble; profitable trade in spices, drugs, and jewels from the Far East and ivory and gold from Africa. The

> *It was clear to everyone, including Octavian himself, that he was now the undisputed master of Rome and the Empire.*
> —HENRY THOMPSON ROWELL
> American historian

Historians usually date the beginning of Octavian's reign as emperor from 28 B.C. In that year, when Octavian formally returned power to the Senate and the people of Rome, he was acclaimed as the restorer of the republic and given the title Augustus.

A wealthy Roman matron makes her way down the Via Appia, or Appian Way, one of the oldest roads in Rome. Determined to make Rome the vital center of a great empire, Augustus ordered the construction of many new roads and the restoration of old roads that were in disrepair.

revenue from all these things was far too valuable to be entrusted to the usual Roman provincial governor who might be tempted, as in the past, to divert funds for his own use. Octavian was determined to use Egypt's revenues to solve the desperate financial problems of Rome.

In the summer of 29 B.C., almost two years after the Battle of Actium, Octavian returned to Rome, where he was greeted by wildly grateful people longing to do him honor. Everywhere he went he was surrounded by robed noblemen, jeweled matrons, ragged beggars, togaed citizens, fishwives, market farmers, and soldiers, all pushing forward to catch a glimpse of him. He was an unlikely conqueror, not thick-necked and muscular like the usual Roman official, but slim, not very tall (although he wore thick soles to add to his height), and rather sickly.

He was pale because he had avoided staying out in the bright Egyptian sun. But he still looked young, his hair (though unkempt) was still blond, his eyes were bright and piercing. He was, as all his many statues show and as recorded by his contemporaries, unusually handsome.

The city gave him a triple triumph — each one more magnificent than Julius Caesar's of 17 years before — for his old conquest of Illyricum, his victory at Actium, and his annexation of Egypt. None of these triumphs celebrated victory over Antony, for a Roman triumphed only over barbarians, and foreigners such as Cleopatra — never over another Roman.

For three days Octavian inspected endless processions of saluting officials, victorious troops with their booty, and thousands of prisoners soon to be slaves. The children of Cleopatra and Antony were paraded before him, next to a float carrying a lifelike image of their dead mother. But Octavian did not enjoy these shows, as Caesar had. In later years he would make some excuse to disappear from such events, but this time he patiently endured it all. The simple honor that pleased him most was the closing of the bronze doors to the ancient temple of Janus, for only the third time since the founding of the city, signifying that peace reigned everywhere within Rome's boundaries.

For the rest of the year Octavian distributed much of his Egyptian income. He paid off his own huge debts, then quadrupled the usual gift of grain to the poor, canceled all unpaid taxes, and gave prize money to every citizen. He dedicated a new Senate

An Egyptian fisherman nets his catch. Afraid that senatorial governors would misuse the vast wealth of Egypt, Augustus retained the country as his personal province and appointed an equestrian governor to rule there as his imperial representative.

house and a magnificent temple to the divine Julius Caesar. He ordered the repair of 82 temples that had fallen into decay. At the same time he treated the city to months of extravagant chariot races, gladiatorial contests, and wild beast shows — in one of which a rhinoceros and a hippopotamus, brought from Egypt and seen in Rome for the first time, were slaughtered to the applause of the crowd.

Octavian did not officiate at any of these later spectacles — partly because they bored him, but also because he was worn out and had to conserve his energies for the tasks ahead. While everybody was celebrating, he rested in his house on the elegant Palatine hill and used the time to think about Rome's problems. He discussed them with his three close advisers: his old friend Agrippa, a great man who proudly took second place although he was more talented than most rulers; the rich and exotic older man Maecenas, whom Octavian teased for his "unguent-dripping curls," but whom he trusted with the most delicate diplomatic errands; and his wife, Livia, whose love and loyalty were indispensable to him and whose advice he took so seriously that throughout his life he made lists of questions

Even after he became emperor, Augustus continued to live in a relatively simple house on the Palatine hill, the site of most of the mansions owned by the richest people in Rome. He also preferred to do much of his business at home.

The Roman plebs greatly enjoyed watching and betting on chariot races, and Augustus sponsored many of them. He personally did not like watching such spectacles, and later, he often refused to officiate at them.

for her. The four spent many long hours in the fall and winter of 28 B.C. sketching out plans for a well-run empire.

Octavian published his goals for all to see and for history to judge: "May it be my privilege to establish the State in a firm and secure position, so as to enjoy the reward of being called the author of the best possible government, and to carry with me when I die the hope that the foundations which I have laid for the State will remain unshaken."

The first issue was what to do about the army — some 60 legions totaling 300,000 men. Octavian knew that the army should not be too big because idle soldiers in the past, led by ambitious generals, had destroyed the stability of the republic. Deciding that 28 legions were enough (along with native auxiliary troops) to guard the 4,000 miles of frontier, he then put them under his direct authority. He now had complete control of the best army in the world.

The soldiers whom he discharged were given no cause to grumble. Octavian was now rich enough to buy them land outright, and he founded 28 new farming towns throughout Italy for these veterans and their families. A direct benefit of this policy was the flowering of the Italian countryside. The new farmers planted olive and fig trees where the land was poor, built small dams and dug ditches for irrigation, fattened thousands of pigs on the acorns of the extensive oak forests, and raised sheep to provide wool for workers' tunics and officials' togas. Later, Octavian founded veterans' colonies outside of Italy from Spain to Syria, picking sites where it was in Rome's interest to have a loyal group of Roman citizens living among the natives. This policy had the indirect benefit of bringing Roman civilization to many primitive communities throughout the empire and was one of Octavian's greatest achievements.

After Octavian had thinned out the army and brought it under his control, he turned his attention to trimming the Senate. Under Julius Caesar, the Senate had swollen in size to 900 and during the Second Triumvirate had increased to nearly 1,000 members. In the turmoil of the last years of the republic and the confused years following Caesar's assassination, the Senate had lost many of its best men. Many current members had bribed their way into it and were completely unqualified. Octavian needed the senators as magistrates to administer the city and the empire. He also wanted the Senate to be a body of men who commanded respect, as in the old days. He dismissed the unqualified senators and encouraged men of better quality to run for senatorial office.

But the most important question remained: What was to be Octavian's official position in the Roman

Augustus' power was ultimately based neither on his constitutional prerogatives nor on his authority, but on the loyalty of the legions which he inherited from his adoptive father.
—A. H. M. JONES
English historian

state? He had been elected consul the last five years in succession and was commander of all the armies and an honorary tribune of the people, but this was an informal and impermanent arrangement that gave no official recognition to his immense power. Octavian did not want to be dictator, and the title of king, with its connotation of ancient tyranny, was out of the question. His title *imperator*, or victorious general, seemed to him too military a term. Although he knew that the Senate and people in their present gratitude would unthinkingly vote him any title he asked for, he also knew the power of Roman tradition, with its deeply rooted belief that Rome was the seat of liberty. Unless he disguised his authority in traditional constitutional forms, it would only be a question of time before some group would conspire against him as they had against Caesar.

After pondering the matter for the rest of the year while the people were still celebrating, he made a brilliantly diplomatic gesture. In January 27 B.C. he suddenly called the senators together and gave them the shock of their lives by announcing that he was resigning everything. He gave back to the Senate and the people of Rome the control of the army, the making of the laws, and the governing of the provinces. By doing this he offered them their ancient republican liberties.

The senators rose from their seats and shouted their dismay. Horrified by the prospect of an empire without Octavian at its head, they implored him to reconsider his decision. They would accept his offer to restore the republic, but Octavian must be its leader.

Octavian at first protested, then, as if reluctant, gave in to their pleading. Elections were immediately called. So great was his popularity that he was once again elected consul and tribune—with the governorships of Gaul, Spain, and Syria thrown in. All of these offices were to be held only at the will of the Senate and the people of Rome, as in the old days of the republic. Everybody wanted to believe that the republic had been restored. Only the most cynical knew it to be a fiction.

Some of the ruins excavated on the Palatine hill. Augustus often brought Agrippa and his other close adviser, Gaius Maecenas, to his home on the Palatine, where they discussed ways to solve the administrative problems of Rome.

Senators proceed to a meeting at the Senate house. Augustus, unwilling to suffer the fate of Julius Caesar, had to avoid being perceived as a dictator by the senators even as he accumulated all the powers necessary for one-man rule of Rome.

The Senate awarded Octavian a crown of oak leaves — the emblem of saving citizens' lives — to hang on his gate, and fresh laurel leaves — the emblem of his victories — to drape around his door. They put a golden shield in the Senate house on which was inscribed a tribute to his "valor, clemency, justice, and piety," character traits most revered by the Romans. Then they discussed what his official title should be. Octavian tactfully suggested the title of *princeps*, which meant "first citizen" or "first among equals." (Much later, the word came to mean prince.)

After days of deliberation the Senate named him *augustus*, which meant blessed, majestic — even sacred. From that day on, Octavian became Augustus Caesar, the name by which history knows him.

As a final honor, the Senate changed the name of the sixth month (Sextilis) to Augustus, just as they had changed the fifth month (Quintilis) to Julius in honor of Julius Caesar (which is why today we have two months named July and August).

The new Augustus now felt free to mold the Roman Empire as he thought best. He later wrote, "I stood before all others in authority, but I had no more actual powers than my colleagues." During his lifetime the consuls and Senate and the people's assemblies proposed and voted on laws as they always had. But Augustus always knew that behind the scenes he had the final say.

The man who does not wish to change the existing political order is a good citizen and a good man.
—AUGUSTUS CAESAR
on the reformed Republic

8

City of Marble

The ruler of the Roman world and its richest man (his private income was greater than all the other revenues collected by the state) lived simply in an old house of local stone and wood on the Palatine. This hill had been a fashionable district since the time that the founder of Rome, the tribal chieftain Romulus, had picked it as the best site for his hut of clay and straw. From then on the most important people in Rome had lived there, building increasingly grand mansions. Augustus, however, disliked pretentious mansions and refused to move into one.

His modest palace must have been crowded and noisy at times, for not only he and his wife, Livia, lived there, but so did her two sons Tiberius and Drusus, his own daughter Julia, and his sister Octavia with her five children. Augustus felt comfortable with children around him. When things got too distracting, he hid in his study at the top of the house.

Augustus was conservative, not to say old-fashioned, in his tastes. He made the women of his family spin and weave in the old-fashioned way, and actually wore the homespun that they produced.
—A. H. M. JONES
English historian

This statue of Emperor Augustus was found near Rome. After securing his position as *princeps*, or first citizen, of Rome Augustus felt free to embark on an extensive program to make Rome into an imperial capital. He later claimed that he had found Rome brick and left it marble.

Although he and Livia gave many private dinners and served imported delicacies and wines, Augustus preferred to eat the simple food of the common people: coarse bread, cottage cheese, lettuce leaves, green figs, and grapes. He nibbled at these snacks all through the day and so would often have no appetite left at his own parties but would simply watch the others eat.

In the afternoon Augustus would rest on a couch in his study, not bothering to remove his clothes and shoes because that would mean wasted time dressing again. He even had two or three barbers cut his hair and shave him at the same time in order to be done with it quickly. After dinner he would go up to his study again and work late on matters of state.

At home Augustus preferred to wear simple clothes and asked his wife, sister, daughter, and later a granddaughter to spin, weave, and sew them for him with their own hands. In his desire to restore old Roman traditions, he was trying to make them act like the proper matrons of the early republic. They humored him and made his clothing but had their own clothes made by dressmakers. He must have kept them busy, because in cold weather he wore four tunics and a heavy gown in addition to an undershirt. Augustus was something of a hypochondriac, worrying constantly about his health. He avoided the sun in winter and summer and never went out on a sunny day without a wide-brimmed hat.

Every morning he received anyone, rich or poor, who came to his house with a petition, putting them at ease with a small joke if they were nervous. Then, if the Senate was in session, he would walk informally to the Senate house through the streets accompanied, inconspicuously, by his bodyguards. He would sit quietly during senatorial debates, and when it was his turn to speak he would allow senators to interrupt him with cries of "I don't understand you!" or "I'd dispute that point if I got the chance!" Occasionally their speeches were so tedious that he would get up to leave, at which they

A Roman consul wears a toga bearing a broad purple stripe, indicating his senatorial status. In order to end corruption in the Senate, Augustus reduced the number of members and supported only men of integrity in the powerful position of consul.

would shout, "We have the right to speak up on things!"

Augustus also took part in city elections, touring the wards with his favorite candidates and casting his vote to show that he still was a man of the people. His masterful, tactful political techniques won for him universal affection. Even though his candidates always won, and the senators voted as they knew he wished, no one felt coerced or patronized. The Senate, although no longer possessing the separate but equal power guaranteed it under the republican constitution, still remained an important political body. Augustus made a habit of consulting groups of senators, working intimately with them and rewarding the best with many important posts

Ruins of the Forum stand in modern Rome. In his quest to turn Rome into an imposing imperial city, Augustus began a massive building program. Ordering huge quantities of pure white marble from nearby Tuscany, Augustus himself financed the erection of many public buildings and monuments.

Perhaps his greatest gift was his political tact. He evidently had a passion for efficiency, but he was careful not to offend public opinion by violent changes, but to work as far as possible within established forms.

—A. H. M. JONES
English historian

and privileges, but he entrusted the administration of the empire to the "new men" of the middle class.

The republic in its last decades had been run by elite groups of senators who rotated consulships, army commands, and provincial governorships among themselves. Augustus put a stop to this practice and its opportunities for favoritism and bribery. He reorganized the government from top to bottom and appointed professional civil servants to run each section. Previously, governors and generals had been allowed to exploit the provincials, keeping for themselves some of the taxes and tribute supposedly destined for Rome. (Julius Caesar had amassed his millions this way.) Augustus put the new governors on fixed salaries and had their tax records sent directly to him to be studied for evidence of graft.

At last all men, including freed slaves, had a chance to be in government service at home or abroad — in charge of finances, taxes, roads, aqueducts, grain distribution, and postal services. Eventually, if they were unusually competent, they might rise to army commands and governorships. The men appointed to the highest posts would afterwards be elected senators for life, entitled to wear a purple stripe on their togas and prestigious gold rings on their fingers. Augustus's program of appointing men of ability was far more liberal and provided far more opportunities to a greater number of people than had the republic in its last years. Perhaps his support of "new men" was so strong because he had started as an outsider himself, an insignificant country relative of one of the ruling groups.

Augustus liked to say that he had found Rome brick and left it marble. This was only partly true, for much would be done by later emperors who tore down entire districts and erected most of the splendid ancient buildings and monuments that survive in Rome today. Nevertheless, Augustus carried out a colossal building program, much of it at his own expense, in which the structures of republican Rome began to vanish beneath those of a new, more elegant imperial city.

Rome had grown in an unplanned, haphazard way. Its streets were narrow, dark, and jammed with traffic. The Tiber River, which ran through the city, was clogged by cave-ins and protruding construction and had become increasingly hard to navigate. The Forum, the heart of the city, was far too crowded. Worst of all, the city's architecture had a dowdy look. Most of its temples and other public structures were built of plain stone in an old-fashioned manner with little ornamentation.

Gradually, beautiful white marble from quarries north of Rome began to replace the bricks, plaster,

This ruin of a Roman aqueduct is located near Rome. Augustus's renovation of Rome included the improvement of the city's vast water-supply system, which was based on a series of huge aqueducts that carried water to Rome.

The Tiber River, which runs through Rome, was the focus of a massive cleanup campaign by Augustus and Agrippa. The river, which by Augustus's time was badly polluted, was cleared of refuse, and its banks were fortified so that barges bearing huge loads could be pulled upriver from the shore.

and ordinary stone of much of the old city. Augustus imported Greek marble workers to teach Roman masons an art in which Greeks had been supreme for centuries. Roman architects soon mastered the use of marble in flowing and elegant ways. Within a single generation there was an obvious gap between the old style and the new. Even private houses were built of marble in the new style. The wealthiest families of Rome were encouraged to contribute to the building program, and many of them funded the restoration or construction of public buildings throughout the city.

Augustus not only changed the appearance of Rome's buildings, but he and Agrippa cleaned up the entire city. They cleared the Tiber River of rubbish and strengthened its banks so that huge ox-drawn barges could haul tons of marble or thousands of bushels of grain up the river to the city's wharves. They rebuilt old city roads, added some new ones, and erected a "Golden Milestone" in the

Forum, which marked the distances from Rome of the chief cities of the empire. They extended and repaired Rome's many aqueducts, beautiful structures that distributed water to more than 700 marble basins for the people's use. Agrippa constructed a huge and hygienic public bath, free to all comers, and also repaired the city's sewer system. One of its many underground pipes, the Cloaca Maxima, was so enormous that he was able to row down its entire length on an inspection trip.

Augustus built an additional forum where legal business could be transacted and juries selected. He encouraged architects in their experiments with concrete faced with brick and had them use this material to build harbor works, aqueducts, and big apartment complexes — the latter relieving Rome's severe housing shortage. Augustus limited the height of the apartments to seven or eight stories, because he wished to discourage speculators from their usual practice of erecting too high tenements of cheap materials that would soon collapse.

He and Agrippa transformed the Field of Mars, a former military training ground, into a glorious park filled with beautiful buildings and grandstands for public entertainments. Augustus chose the far north end of this area as the site of his mausoleum, a huge circular building. At the opposite end he erected the theater of Marcellus, enough of which stands today to impart a sense of its scale and elegance. Inside the park was a huge chart of the world prepared by government geographers, and although it had Asia and Africa joined together and bordered by indefinite oceans and "unknown" lands, it proudly showed the entire Roman Empire with its vast network of connecting roads. As a backdrop to the magnificence of the park stood the seven hills of the city, shining with white buildings and bronze rooftops — a setting, as the visiting Greek geographer Strabo said, "for great deeds and men."

In 27 B.C., when he was 36 years old, Augustus left Agrippa in charge and departed for Spain with his oldest stepson, Tiberius, then 15 years old. Spain's provinces were among Rome's oldest and most civilized, but they still contained many un-

I realize that you care not only about the common life of men but also about providing suitable public buildings to express the majesty of your empire.
—VITRUVIUS
architect of Augustus,
in his dedication
to Augustus

conquered savage tribes in the interior hills. Augustus spent months with Roman officials on the coast and then with Roman troops as they bloodily subdued the hill tribes. He ordered a massive network of roads to crisscross Spain from end to end. Many of these roads made of fitted stones were remarkable feats of engineering, carved out of rocky mountainsides and crossing Spain's steep canyons on arched stone bridges. Intended primarily for military transport, these great roads soon became peaceful trade routes, carrying Spain's vast mineral wealth of silver, iron, lead, and copper from the interior to the coast. At strategic points Augustus established veterans' colonies that in a few years became important towns and centers of Roman in-

Ruins from the Augustan Forum of the late 1st century B.C. can be found beneath more modern structures. Augustus built his forum at one end of the main Forum as a place to conduct legal business and select juries.

fluence. He ordered the conquered hill tribes to be moved down into the valleys where they would forget their wild ways and become a productive part of community life.

Augustus's three years in Spain undermined his health, and after returning home in 23 B.C. he suddenly became very ill. The Senate and people were frantic at the prospect of his death, fearing that civil wars would again erupt among those who wanted to succeed him. Lying gaunt and weak on what many expected to be his deathbed, Augustus summoned his most important advisers and made a farewell speech. He then handed his signet ring marked with a sphinx head to his friend Agrippa as a sign that he thought him the most qualified man to run the Roman Empire — although he meticulously left that selection to the Senate. Fortunately for Rome — because Agrippa had made too many political enemies to ensure a smooth transition — Augustus's doctor, a Greek freedman, ordered cold-water treatments instead of Augustus's usual sweat baths and rubdowns. Somehow this drastic treatment worked, and by midsummer he was back on his feet.

Augustus had many times surprised his family, friends, and enemies by surviving the severe illnesses that had plagued him from childhood. No one had expected him to live this long — to almost the age of 40. But he was to surprise the world further by living almost another 40 years, years that were of equal greatness and achievement.

9

"Dismiss Me from the Stage"

Augustus's amazing longevity and his continued wise management of the empire would ensure that the Roman system of government he had molded would endure for centuries. But at the time of his close brush with death in his fortieth year there was no one who could know this. In fact, it seemed reasonable to assume that at any moment he could be sick again and this time not recover.

Augustus's choice of successor was, therefore, a matter of supreme importance. The passing on of one's power to one's sons was a long-held tradition of aristocratic Roman families, but Augustus had no sons. On what he had thought was his deathbed Augustus had handed Agrippa his signet ring, but that was surely an act of desperation, for Augustus knew that rule by a self-made man from an unimportant family would be difficult for Roman nobles to accept. The only way to avoid the civil wars that

Augustus, of course, left his mark upon the entire Roman world, and his reorganization of the Empire, so radical that he may well be considered its founder, was his greatest and most enduring feat.
—HENRY THOMPSON ROWELL
American historian

Emperor Augustus gives his directions for provincial government to a general assembly of the Gauls in France. Augustus established an imperial bureaucracy that standardized Roman rule in the provinces and oversaw the smooth transaction of daily business.

could once again tear the empire apart would be to find a direct male descendent of Augustus's own blood, and the sole chance of that would be through his only child, his daughter Julia.

Augustus proposed what he thought would be an ideal solution: a marriage between Julia and Agrippa. Julia was a flighty, spoiled 17-year-old, and Agrippa was a serious, hardworking 40-year-old executive. The wide difference in their characters and ages and the fact that Agrippa was already married were of no consideration to Augustus, who had high hopes that their union would provide him with the grandsons he needed to succeed him. Agrippa agreed to divorce his wife, and Julia had little choice but to obey her father.

Augustus then left Rome on another three-year inspection trip, this time to the eastern half of the empire. He traveled through the Greek-speaking provinces of Asia Minor (modern Turkey), then

The presence of a Roman amphitheater in Macedonia, Yugoslavia, shows the extent of Roman influence during the Augustan Age. Roman customs were brought to the provinces mainly by soldiers, who often married local women and settled there, spreading Roman civilization throughout the Mediterranean.

southward to Syria and on to Judea, whose King Herod was a Roman ally. He met with Roman governors and rulers of buffer states subordinate to Rome, removing them if he found them incompetent or untrustworthy, listening to their complaints, and adjusting their tribute or taxes.

The prosperous and civilized cities along the fertile eastern Mediterranean coast were of great importance to the Roman Empire. They welcomed Augustus as their monarch, and in return he gave them new buildings, forums, and roads. He received ambassadors from many lands — even one from distant India who presented him with the Western world's first tiger.

Beyond the desert kingdoms to the east were the warlike Parthians whose excellent cavalry sometimes crossed the Euphrates River on raids. Augustus ordered high-towered observation posts and forts to be built at these crossings, but when the Roman Senate urged him to go further and attack Parthia itself, he sent them word to be satisfied with the lands they already had.

On his way back to Rome he met with the empire's greatest poet, Vergil, who read to him the long epic poem, the *Aeneid*, which Augustus had commissioned. Of all the great Latin writers who flourished in the Augustan Age — men such as the historian Livy and the poets Ovid and Horace — Vergil was the greatest. The *Aeneid* told the story of the "lords of everything, the toga'd people." It spoke for all Romans, who felt that Rome stood on the brink of a magnificent dream, an orderly rule, a peaceful empire without end in territory or time, and that the gods themselves wished for such a leader and such an empire. "We shall learn to forget fear," sang the *Aeneid*, "a new generation, a golden race, a glorious age is beginning." Another of its famous passages expressed a Roman ideal:

> Remember, Roman, your task is to rule nations
> And your genius shall be to lead men into peace
> To be generous to the conquered and to stand
> Firm against the proud.

The oppressive affection that the "father of the country" bestowed on Rome was not unlike the affection he thought he was giving his daughter [Julia], in the sense that one and the other were thereby deprived of any free will.
—GILBERT CHARLES PICARD
French historian

In this 19th-century painting, Emperor Augustus listens to the poet Vergil read his *Aeneid*. Considered one of the greatest works of classical Latin literature, the *Aeneid* is an epic poem that tells the story of the founding of Rome.

Augustus returned to Rome in 19 B.C., entering quietly into the city by night to avoid an elaborate public welcome. His daughter, Julia, proudly showed him his year-old grandson, Gaius. Soon afterward a second grandson, Lucius, was born. With joy he adopted both as his sons and gave them the name of Caesar.

For the next two years in his small office on the Palatine hill he worked incessantly on the problems of his huge empire. Then, wanting to see at firsthand the important provinces in Gaul (France), he asked the Senate to confirm Agrippa as his co-regent for the next five years. They agreed, comfortable with a system that reminded them of the two ruling co-consuls of the former republic. They also recognized that in the event of Augustus's death,

Agrippa would be an excellent regent until Gaius came of age.

Augustus's inspection trip to Gaul in 16 B.C. was his last inspection trip outside of Italy. He took with him his stepson, Livia's 25-year-old son Tiberius. As he debarked from his sailing ship at the port of Fréjus, on the southern coast, he recognized some aging hulks that once were part of Cleopatra's fleet that he had captured 15 years before.

He stopped for a while at Nîmes, a big town and a veterans' colony, where he built a small temple. (The temple has survived in such perfect condition that Thomas Jefferson studied it when he needed a model for the Virginia House of Burgesses.) Agrippa had preceded Augustus in Nîmes and while there had completed one of the most impressive triumphs of all Roman architecture, the 900-foot *Pont du Gard*, a bridge over a steep river valley, part of the aqueduct that carried water to the colony. Some of the stone blocks of this many-arched bridge weighed two tons and had been lifted by cranes and fitted over wooden forms some 150 feet above the Gard River — a staggering feat of engineering and design.

After spending some time in Nîmes, Augustus traveled north to Lugdunum (Lyons), a small army town he picked as an ideal spot from which to administer the other, less settled provinces of Gaul. He spent three years in Lyons. Although Augustus reorganized Gaul's inefficient financial structure, he was careful not to interfere with tribal customs and religious rites or even with local governments. Instead, he concentrated on establishing new colonies, spreading the learning of the Latin language, and building great trunk roads that spread out in all directions, connected in turn by Gaul's network of wide, slow rivers. Over this excellent communication and transportation system passed the country's produce: beer, hams, geese, wool cloth, cheeses, leather, carrots (a luxury), glass, and pottery for export all over the empire. The Gauls, like the Spaniards, quickly became romanized. Augustus's benign treatment of Gaul was one of his foremost achievements.

The Roman historian Livy was one of the many writers sponsored by Augustus. Imperial patronage of the arts, especially of literature, encouraged an explosion of creative talent during the Augustan Age.

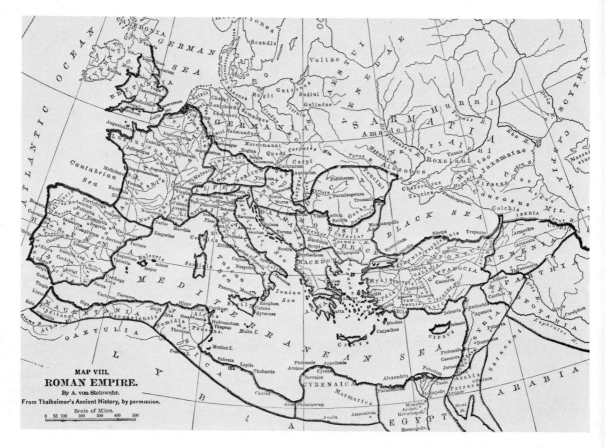

MAP VIII.
ROMAN EMPIRE.
By A. von Steinwehr.
From Thalheimer's Ancient History, by permission.

Scale of Miles.
0 50 100   200   300   400   500

The extent of the Roman Empire at the end of Augustus's reign. Augustus added more territory to the Roman state than any ruler before or after him. His biggest failure was in Germany, where the destruction of three Roman legions in 9 B.C. forced him to withdraw to the Rhine River, where the empire's border would remain.

Another achievement with far-reaching effects was his extension of the empire and the establishment of safe frontiers. During his three years in Gaul, Augustus and his generals worked out a grand strategy to deal with hostile barbarian tribes from the Alps to the North Sea. They decided to move the frontier northward to the Danube River and eastward to the Rhine. This decision covered a tremendous territory, comprising modern Switzerland, Austria, parts of Hungary, and the Balkans. In addition, to guard a weak stretch between the sources of the two rivers, they planned to advance later into the land of the Germans — the only part of the strategy that would end in disaster.

In 15 B.C. the campaign opened, conducted by Augustus's extremely able young stepsons, Tiberius and Drusus. By the time Augustus left Gaul two years later they had successfully conquered tribes from the Alps to the Danube and were on their way north to conquer the rest. These extensions of territory, masterminded by Augustus and his young generals, were the greatest of any Roman emperor. Horace sang that the empire stretched from the sun's rising to its setting in the west.

The Senate commemorated Augustus's safe return to Rome by dedicating an altar to the peace he had achieved for so many millions. Peace to the Romans meant peace within their borders and included the concept of growth and pacification. Augustus was always careful to calculate the benefits of war, keeping the idea of internal peace foremost in his mind. He did not enjoy the risks of war and did not undertake it if he thought war would weaken the resources of the state.

Roman cavalrymen bear battle standards. To gain the favor of the Philippi veterans, Octavian broke up large landed estates into farms that were given to the soldiers for their service to him. By this action, Octavian created a new base of support throughout the Italian countryside.

That same year the Senate elected him *Pontifex Maximus* (chief priest) in a ceremony watched by the biggest crowd the city had ever seen. Augustus took his priestly role very seriously, trying to encourage reverence for the gods and to reform the upper class's loose morality, but he was not very successful.

In the spring of 12 B.C. Agrippa suddenly died, an unexpected blow for Augustus. Three years later his popular stepson Drusus was thrown from his horse in Germany and died of his injuries. Within a year Maecenas, Augustus's most reliable adviser, was also dead. It was the beginning of a long and lonely period, for Augustus would outlive all his old friends and most of his family. He spent more time than

This bronze statue, part of the permanent collection at the Metropolitan Museum of Art in New York City, is from the Augustan period. Though opinions differ as to whether it is a statue of Lucius or Gaius Caesar, most experts agree that it is probably of the young Gaius.

Emperor Augustus died in the summer of A.D. 14. Because he and Livia had no children and his favorite grandsons had both died, Augustus had been forced to promote as his successor his stepson Tiberius. Although a capable officer and administrator, Tiberius never won Augustus's confidence.

ever with his two grandsons, doting on them and spoiling them dangerously. The Senate, aware that Augustus was grooming the boys as his successors, proposed that the older one, Gaius, be made a senator at the age of 15. Then, seeing that Augustus was pleased, the Senate added that Gaius should become a consul when he reached 20. Soon thereafter after they awarded the same honors to the younger boy.

About this time there occurred an ordinary event — Augustus's decree that a tax census should be taken in King Herod's kingdom of Judea. This decree became famous later because, according to the Christian Bible, it brought Joseph and his wife, Mary, from Nazareth to Bethlehem, where she gave birth to a son, fulfilling a messianic prophecy in the Jewish Bible. King Herod, upon hearing of the birth of the Messiah, the King of the Jews, ordered a massacre of all infant boys. One who escaped was Joseph and Mary's son, Jesus Christ, who was to bring about a greater change in the Roman Empire than any other man. But at the time his birth was of only the slightest significance. The Christian practice of dividing dates into B.C. (before Christ) and A.D. (*Anno Domini*, the year of our Lord) was never adopted by the Romans. To Augustus, the year of Christ's birth was 753 A.U.C..

Augustus (being crowned) and the goddess Roma, patroness of the city of Rome, receive Tiberius (left) as Augustus's successor. Upon his death, Augustus was deified, as Julius Caesar had been. The deification of his stepfather ensured a smooth transition to power for Tiberius.

Few rulers in world history have managed public affairs as well as Augustus, but in his own home he was not so successful. His modest wants, self-discipline, and rectitude were not easy to live with, and his daughter Julia reacted strongly. Having borne five children to Agrippa to fulfill her father's dynastic plans, she had had enough. Her defiant, wild behavior with many lovers became notorious. After a particularly offensive episode (she staged an orgy in one of the most sacred places in Rome), Augustus banished her to a small island for the rest of her life. They never saw each other again. A few years later he banished Julia's daughter, also named Julia, for immoral behavior, and put to death her lover, her husband, and her infant son born in banishment. Augustus's fifth grandchild, a retarded boy, became so vicious and uncontrolled that he, too, was exiled.

In 2 B.C. Augustus was awarded the title of *Pater Patriae*, or "Father of His Country." With tears in his eyes he thanked the Senate, saying that he prayed he could keep their approval to his dying day. The title was heartfelt. To the Romans a father was a figure of respect and power. Augustus seemed to be almost a supernatural father to his people. The sight of his face, still remarkably handsome, and his slim, still graceful figure, had an enormous effect on them; he was monarch, priest, and father, all in one.

Now Augustus centered all his hopes and affection on his two eldest grandsons. But in a few years both were dead, one from battle wounds, the other from disease. They were mourned by millions of citizens who had seen in their youthful features another young Augustus.

Augustus was inconsolable. Livia's son Tiberius, in his late forties, was finally made his heir and successor in A.D. 4, but neither man could pretend it was done with any affection or pleasure. By now Tiberius was disappointed and bitter. He had served his stepfather loyally and had been a brilliant field commander, but he had been repeatedly passed over in favor of Augustus's blood relatives, no matter how incompetent.

In A.D. 6 there were sudden tribal uprisings in the north, and Tiberius quickly left for the front. He put down most of the trouble with a great pincerlike sweep, but in A.D. 9 the Roman general Publius Quintilius Varus, a former governor who had never bothered to learn about the German land and people and had taxed them heavily, was led with three legions into ambush in the deep forest of Teutoburg, miles across the Rhine, and massacred. The legions' eagle standards were captured, a terrible disgrace to Rome. When another Roman commander reached the battle site, he found the whitening bones of men and horses, and human heads fastened to tree trunks.

Augustus was shattered by this news. He refused to cut his hair or shave for months and often banged

This bronze statue of Augustus stands in modern Rome. Inscribed on the pedestal is one of the many titles awarded to Augustus — and one of the few he readily accepted: *Pater Patriae,* **Father of His Country.**

his head on a door, shouting, "Quintilius Varus, give me back my legions!" He was through with expansion and wrote to Tiberius to pull the frontier back to the west side of the Rhine and keep it there. This momentous decision meant that the Germans were never romanized, as the Gauls and the Spaniards had been. Today, the boundary between the countries that speak Germanic languages and the countries that speak languages based on Latin is almost the same as the boundary that Augustus established.

Augustus had become a very old man. He walked with a limp, and his eyesight had grown weak. His right hand was often numb, but this did not prevent him from writing down in A.D. 14 (at the age of 75) a long record of his achievements, which he wished to have proclaimed by the Senate upon his death.

"At the age of 19," the old emperor proudly began, "at my own expense, I raised an army and liberated the Republic from the oppression of tyrants. . . . After extinguishing the civil wars, although in supreme possession of the whole empire, I transferred the Republic from my own power to the free control of the Senate and the people of Rome."

He went on to list his victories, his gifts to the people, the entertainments he had paid for, the treaties and laws he had made, the colonies he had founded, the defeated kings and princes who had been led before his chariot at triumphs.

Later that year, in August (his name month), he lay dying in a country house in the same room in which his own father had died. Livia, his wife of 52 years, and her son Tiberius — the next emperor — were at his side. He called for a mirror and had his hair combed and his jaw set straight. Then he quoted the lines used at the end of Roman comedies:

> Since well I've played my part,
> Clap now your hands and with applause
> Dismiss me from the stage.

He murmured farewell to Livia, the only person left in his empire for him to love, and asked her to remember their many days together. Afterward, Tiberius had the emperor's proud record inscribed in bronze and placed in temples throughout the empire. To Augustus's words Tiberius added this preface:

> Here below is written a record of the exploits of the divine Augustus by which he brought the world under the empire of the Roman people.

> *The Golden Age of Augustus was not merely a propaganda trick; it was a reality.*
> —PAUL MACKENDRICK
> historian

Further Reading

Braund, David. *Augustus to Nero: A Sourcebook on Roman History*. Sydney, Australia: Croom Helm, 1985.

Brooks, P. S. and N. Z. Walworth. *When the World Was Rome*. Philadelphia: Lippincott, 1972.

Bruns, Roger. *Julius Caesar*. New York: Chelsea House, 1987.

Earl, D. *The Age of Augustus*. New York: Crown, 1968.

Firth, John B. *Augustus Caesar*. New York: Putnam, 1902.

Hoobler, Dorothy, and Thomas Hoobler. *Cleopatra*. New York: Chelsea House, 1986.

Horace. *The Essential Horace*. Translated by Burton Raffel. San Francisco: North Point Press, 1983.

Jones, A. H. M. *Augustus*. London: Chatto & Windus, 1970.

Kittredge, Mary. *Marc Antony*. New York: Chelsea House, 1988.

Picard, Gilbert-Charles. *Augustus and Nero*. New York: Crowell, 1965.

Rowell, H. T. *Rome in the Augustan Age*. Norman: University of Oklahoma Press, 1985.

Shakespeare, William. *Antony and Cleopatra*. New York: Penguin, 1981.

———. *Julius Caesar*. New York: Penguin, 1981.

Starr, C. G. *The Ancient Romans*. New York: Oxford University Press, 1971.

———. *The Roman Empire: A Study in Survival*. New York: Oxford University Press, 1982.

Starr, Chester D. *Civilization and the Caesars*. Ithaca: Cornell University Press, 1954.

Suetonius. *The Twelve Caesars*. Translated by R. Graves. New York: Penguin, 1967.

Vergil. *Georgics*. Translated by L. P. Wilkinson. New York: Penguin, 1983.

———. *The Aeneid*. Translated by Robert Fitzgerald. New York: Random House, 1983.

Chronology

63 B.C.	Born Gaius Octavius (known in English as Octavian)
March 44	Julius Caesar is assassinated; his will declares Octavian his heir, giving him the name Caesar
April 43	Octavian is elected consul
43	Forms Second Triumvirate with Antony and Lepidus
42	Antony and Octavian defeat the conspirators at Philippi and divide the Roman Empire between them
	Antony meets Cleopatra VII, queen of Egypt
41	Octavian marries Scribonia
40	Antony marries Octavia, sister of Octavian
38	Octavian divorces Scribonia and marries Livia
37	Antony returns to Egypt; Cleopatra agrees to back his Parthian expedition
36	Antony bigamously marries Cleopatra; his Parthian campaign ends in failure
	Octavian defeats Sextus Pompey in Sicily
32	Antony sails for Greece, accompanied by Cleopatra and her fleet; formally divorces Octavia
	Octavian declares war on Cleopatra
31	Octavian defeats Antony and Cleopatra at Actium
30	Antony and Cleopatra commit suicide; Octavian annexes Egypt
29	Octavian returns to Rome
27	Restores the Republic and is given the name Augustus
22	Augustus arranges the marriage of his daughter, Julia, to Agrippa
19	Adopts Gaius and Lucius, sons of Julia and Agrippa, and gives them the name Caesar
16	Leaves for Gaul accompanied by his stepson Tiberius
12	Returns to Rome; Senate elects him Pontifex Maximus (chief priest)
	Agrippa dies suddenly
A.D. 4	Augustus names Tiberius heir and successor following the death of Lucius and Gaius
14	Dies at age 75

Index

Nancy Zinsser Walworth is a graduate of Smith College and holds an M.A. from Radcliffe. She is coauthor of *When the World Was Rome, The World of Walls*, and *The World Awakes*. A mother of four and grandmother of five, she resides with her husband in New Canaan, Connecticut.

Arthur M. Schlesinger, jr., taught history at Harvard for many years and is currently Albert Schweitzer Professor of the Humanities at City University of New York. He is the author of numerous highly praised works in American history and has twice been awarded the Pulitzer Prize. He served in the White House as special assistant to Presidents Kennedy and Johnson.

PICTURE CREDITS

Art Resource: pp. 20, 56, 57, 69, 74, 79, 86, 87, 92; The Bettmann Archive: pp. 2, 12, 14, 15, 19, 21, 22, 23, 24, 28, 30, 32, 33, 34, 36, 37, 38, 39, 40, 41, 46, 49, 50, 52, 54, 55, 60, 62, 65, 66, 68, 72, 73, 80, 82, 89, 90, 96, 98, 99, 100, 101, 104, 105; Culver Pictures: pp. 16, 17, 18, 31, 42, 44, 45, 47, 48, 58, 64, 70, 76, 85, 94, 103; Metropolitan Museum of Art: p. 102; Scala/Art Resource: pp. 26, 75